/

FACTS
Dumfries
1981

The only method of reaching the Calf of Man is by boat. Here The Sunbeam enters Cow Harbour.

# The Calf of Man

### W. LOCKINGTON MARSHALL
*with photographs by the Author*

SHEARWATER PRESS

DOUGLAS ISLE OF MAN

## Dedication

To the Manx people and to all who love the Island this book is dedicated.

The Author's royalties are to be donated to The Manx Museum and National Trust.

## Acknowledgements

The Author acknowledges with gratitude the assistance that he has received from the following—without their help this book could not have been written:—

L. Anderson, Mrs. T. Clague, I. Crowe, A. M. Cubbon, O.B.E., B.A., F.S.A., F.M.A., Miss Gibb, Miss A. M. Harrison, B.A., and the staff of the Manx Museum, E. F. Ladds, B.A. The Douglas Public Library, H. D. C. MacLeod, M.H.K., J. Maddrell, Mrs. H. S. Proctor, J. Robson, Deputy Secretary, The Northern Lighthouse Board, Sir Ralph Stevenson, G.C.M.G., Mrs. L. Viol, Lieutenant-Commander and Mrs. Frank Williams, M. Wright, the Warden on the Calf, The staff of the General Registry of Deeds, The Manx Museum and National Trust.

ISBN 0 904980 19 7

Printed in the Isle of Man
by Bridson & Horrox Limited,
for Shearwater Press Limited,
Welch House, Church Road,
Onchan, Isle of Man.

# Contents

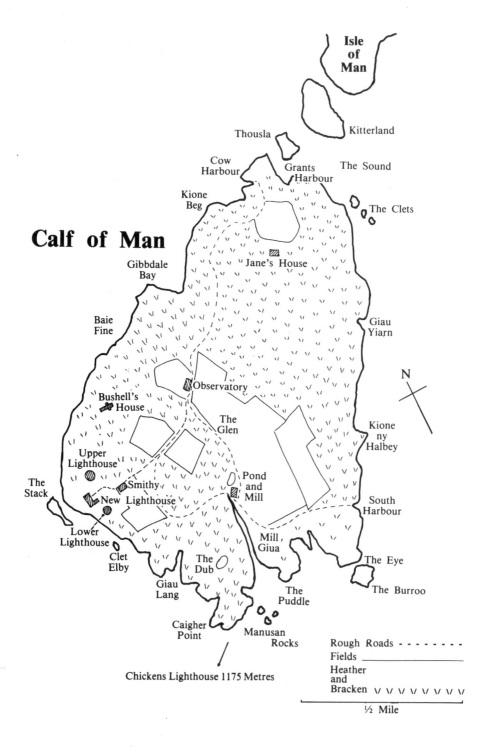

Isle
of
Man

Kitterland

Thousla

The Sound

Cow
Harbour

Grants
Harbour

Kione
Beg

The Clets

**Calf of Man**

Gibbdale
Bay

Jane's House

Baie
Fine

Giau
Yiarn

Observatory

Bushell's
House

The
Glen

Upper
Lighthouse

Kione
ny
Halbey

The
Stack

Smithy

Pond
and
Mill

New
Lighthouse

South
Harbour

Lower
Lighthouse

Clet
Elby

Mill
Giua

The
Dub

The Eye

Giau
Lang

The
Puddle

The Burroo

Caigher
Point

Manusan
Rocks

N

Rough Roads - - - - - - - -

Fields _____

Heather
and
Bracken  ᴠ ᴠ ᴠ ᴠ ᴠ ᴠ ᴠ ᴠ

Chickens Lighthouse 1175 Metres

½ Mile

# CHAPTER 1

## A GENERAL DESCRIPTION
## AND
## GEOLOGY

The Calf of Man has had several names. The Norsemen called it *Kalfr,* meaning a small island near to a larger one. In the Manorial Roll of 1511 it is called Le Calf; the Manx equivalent to that was Yn Calloo. The Manx fishermen had, however, a different name for it. To them it was *Yn Kellagh*—The Cock.

This small island is separated from the south-western extremity of the Isle of Man by a dangerous strip of sea about a quarter of a mile wide, called the Sound, or, in Manx, Yn Keelis. The name given to it by Joseph Train in his history written in 1845 was 'The Race'. This may not have been accurate but it was a very good description, for the current through the Sound at times runs at no less than eight knots.

The Calf is about five miles round the coast, one and a half miles long from north-east to south-west, and about one mile across the centre of that axis. Its area is 616½ acres, 490 of these being heath and foreshore and 126½ acres pasture and once-arable land. The highest point of the island, 421 feet, is on the north coast. The Calf is surrounded by almost continuous cliffs, the highest being Oirr Vooar which is 400 feet.

There are four so-called harbours or landing places. Cow Harbour just across the Sound consists of a slipway and a disused boathouse. It has this name because when the island was farmed cattle used to be made to swim across to the harbour at slack water. They were fastened to a rowing boat, by a rope from the stern to their horns, in order to guide them safely to the landing on the other side. Grant's and Carey's Harbours have small concrete landing stages, in gullies just a few hundred yards south-east of Cow Harbour; they are used at different states of the tide. The principal landing place is called South Harbour. It is situated at the southern end of the south-east coast, and here the lighthouse keepers and their stores are landed. There is a small store shed, probably built at the same time as the first lighthouse, and a concrete jetty. This landing place is probably the most sheltered on the Calf, if any can be described as such!

The most popular way of reaching the Calf is from Port Erin to either Cow, Carey's, or Grant's Harbours—this is the shortest route. Some people travel from Port St. Mary to South Harbour because of the magnificent coastal scenery to be enjoyed as the boat passes the Chasms and the Sugarloaf Rock on the main island. The whole system is, however, very uncertain as it depends entirely upon wind and tide. Conditions can change so rapidly, that within a short time of landing, the swell can make it almost impossible for a boat to remain alongside for sufficient time to let the passengers re-embark. On many occasions people misjudge their step and fall. There always seems to be a swell in the Sound even on the calmest day and it is not unknown for visitors to have had their stay on the Calf extended overnight!

In addition to the inlets used as landing places there are several others. These are called in Manx 'Giau'. Going clockwise round the calf from the Sound, the first is Giau Yiarn, in roughly the middle of the east coast. Then in the centre of the south coast is Mill Giau, into which the mill stream used to run and which ultimately opens out into the Puddle. To the south of the west coast is Giau Lang. At the head of the inlet which is south of the lighthouses is a small cave, which completely dries out at low tide. In the roof of the cave is what appears to be a man-made vertical shaft roughly thirty feet high which reaches right through the rock. Near the opening at the top of the shaft on the rough land above the cave is a vertical stone about three feet high. The story is that smugglers used to fasten a lantern on to the stone to guide their boats into the cave and the goods were then drawn up the shaft. Another explanation for the existence of the shaft is that it was connected with mining in some way.

There are two bays on the island, The Puddle in the south and almost opposite on the north coast Gibbdale Bay which is surrounded by magnificent cliffs. There are four islets off the Calf, Kitterland and Thousla in the Sound. The Burroo due south, and the Stack due east. Kitterland, the largest islet, is of low lying rock. It has about one acre of rough pasture upon it. Its name is supposed to have been derived from a legendary Viking chieftain called Kitter. Thousla is little more than a rock. Situated upon it is a concrete structure surmounted by an iron cross. The Burroo, from the Scandinavian word 'Borg', meaning a small round hill, is separated from the Calf by the Goll-ny-Vurroo. A "Goll" is a course or channel. At very low tide the Burroo can be reached on foot, and right through it is an opening called The Eye. The Stack is formed of semi-crystalline basalt rock. It is in the form of two pyramids, about 100 feet high and is near the lighthouses across the Goll-ny-Staggy. It gets its name from another Norse word 'Stakkr', meaning a pile of hay. There are several dangerous rocks off the Calf. The Clets are to the north-east, at the southern end of the Sound. The best known rock, however, is the Chickens Rock, 1275 yards to the south-west of the Calf.

The principal road is very worn and rough, only a pair of wheel tracks in places, just suitable for the vehicle used by the lighthouse keepers. The road starts at Cow Harbour and runs steeply uphill, and then almost due west for about 500 yards. It then turns south-west, with a magnificent view of the cliffs at Gibbdale Bay. The road then goes past the old farmhouse, now the bird observatory, where it divides. One arm continues south-west for about 250 yards before turning west, past the remains of the smithy, to the two old lighthouses and the recently erected one. This part of the road is about one and a quarter miles long. After dividing at the Observatory, the other arm of the road turns almost due south, passing once-cultivated areas on the left hand and a marsh and mill dam on the right. At this point it is joined by another track from the lighthouses, and continues past the ruins of the mill for a further 200 yards. The track then turns east for 250 yards, and then south-east for a further 200, to South Harbour. This track from the Observatory to South Harbour is about three-quarters of a mile in length. In addition to the main tracks mentioned there are one or two footpaths.

There are several buildings on the Calf. From the Isle of Man looking across the Sound a ruined house can be seen situated towards the top of the north-east hillside. This is Jane's House. It is shown on the Richard Wilson map of 1771 as the 'Mansion House'. The present structure dates from about 1890 when it was rebuilt. There is a small quarry at the back from which the stone was obtained. It is a two-storied house, with two rooms downstairs and another in the roof space. Outside, there is a yard with outhouses. As it is now many years since it was last occupied, its state of preservation is remarkable. Much of the slate roof is still in position, and it is possible, though not very prudent, to climb the staircase. The attic room still has its wooden floor; it receives light from a glazed iron skylight. Some of the doors and woodwork remain, and there are the remains of a fireplace. As Jane's House is so high up the slope, obtaining water would have caused a problem if it had not been for seepage from a marshy area nearby. The presence of the water probably dictated the position of the house. The last people to live there were a group of labourers who were employed in building a new dock at Cow Harbour in the early part of this century.

Just north of the centre of the island, in a small sheltered valley on the track to the lighthouses, is the bird observatory building, once the farmhouse. Further along the road is the ruin of a smithy, and at the end, on the western side of the island, stand the two old lighthouses and the modern one. The only other building of any size is the 19th century mill. This is situated on the track that runs from the Observatory to South Harbour. It is now roofless, and one of the only pair of stones lies broken nearby. The mill obtained its water from a millpond with a dam. The water supply must have been rather uncertain as there is no river and the pond is fed from a marsh and a seepage spring. In 1818 a small limekiln was also built, probably by the lighthouse keepers who farmed a small area around the lights. On the north-west coast on the highest and most exposed place on the island, are the foundations of a building called Bushell's House.

There are several marshy areas on the Calf, and also a small pond called by the Manx a "Dub". In this case the water lies in an area from which peat has been extracted for fuel.

Apart from the small quarry at Jane's House which has already been mentioned, there is also a quarry behind the Observatory, from which the stone for that building came. The builders were fortunate in finding such a ready supply of material, for in addition to the quarries there is a gravel pit west-southwest of Jane's House. The most recent use for this was in the construction of the new lighthouse.

There are two references to peculiar pillars on the Calf, but a careful search has failed to find them on the ground. Richard Townley in "A Journal kept in the Isle of Man", dated 1791, described how he landed "at the north end", and went on to say, "There were three or four pointed rocks at the place where we landed that presented a most grotesque yet most beautiful appearance. The upper parts of them are formed of a kind of shining spar as white as virgin snow, the lower a kind of bastard marble as black as jet, and they are exactly divided about the middle height, as to have the most exact resemblance of one pillar having been fixed by art upon another." David Robertson in his book *A Tour through the Isle of Man* dated 1794 (three years later), found them in an entirely different place! He wrote "Near the middle of the Calf there are three pointed pillars, which from their novelty claimed our attention, one half from the base being black bastard marble, and the other of shining spar, white as the new fallen snow." There may, of course, have been pillars in both places. On the other hand Robertson may have read the account in Townley's book and added the pillars to enliven a rather dull account of his ramble on the island.

The amateur geologist visiting the Calf will find the geological features to be of great interest. Professor W. Boyd-Dawkins, together with other authorities, states that the Calf and the Chickens Rock are part of the general north-east to south-west axis of the Isle of Man which extends into the Lake District of Cumberland in one direction, and the Mountains of Mourne in Ireland in the other. This is part of an enormous area of rocks formed of petrified sand and gravel under the sea. These banks were between 30,000 and 40,000 feet thick, and the tremendous pressure compacted the sand beds into sandstone. In the same way, the mud and fine material were formed into a type of slate called "Cerite Schist". This schist, while being consolidated, was subjected to forces which not only broke and crumbled it, but contorted and folded it so that the strata were no longer horizontal. Examples of this can be seen in many places. A trip along the Marine Drive from Douglas to Port Soderick on the main island shows this to perfection.

Parts of this material were much softer than others, so the action of the sea carved the present shape of the Isle of Man as it destroyed the softer areas. This action was also carried on by the erosion of the wind and rain, and by the glaciers grinding away the softer rocks and leaving the harder ones. The rocks were also traversed by lines of weakness. The Sound between the Isle of Man and the Calf is considered to have been one of these lines which ultimately enabled the sea to break through. Immediately southwest of the reef upon which the Chickens Rock lighthouse is built, the sea plunges down to one of the deepest parts of the Irish Sea. Some authorities are of the opinion that this subsidence must have played a part in the separation of the Calf from the main island.

The area of slate that forms the Calf was acted upon by the glaciers which stripped off any other rock formations such as limestone, just as it did on most parts of the Isle of Man. Much clayey drift with slaty debris has been deposited on the Calf as the glaciers melted. There is a large area of this material both south and east of the farm. Without this, of course, there would not have been any arable land. The soil on the rest of the Calf, apart from one or two patches of gravel, is very shallow. An examination of the Geological Survey Map of 1892-97, will show how closely the old arable farmland followed the outlines of this area of glacial drift.

J. G. Cummings, in his book *The Isle of Man,* written in 1848, describes a section of the gravel deposits. "Near the eastern pile of stones which has been erected upon an eminence of 400 feet above the level of the sea, is a very remarkable deposit of boulders, gravel and sand. It is about 100 yards north of the pile, and at twenty-eight feet lower elevation, but still resting on, and covering in the shape of an oblong spheroidal, and somewhat raised portion of the clay schist which forms the substratum of the islet. A good section has been made into the very heart of this mass (which is about thirteen feet deep and fifty feet across in the longer i.e. the north and south axis) for the purpose of procuring gravel for the neighbouring road, and exhibits a somewhat irregular yet distinct stratification, which consists in the lowest part of a deposit of fine sand, above that patches of gravel in sand, then still higher up of gravel and scratched fragments of rock, and good sized boulders, and the rocks are not any of them, such as we could swear to as belonging to the immediate locality. There are red and grey Syenites, Porphyries, Granites, Grits, and Sandstone, either from Cumberland or the south of Scotland, but not a fragment as far as I have hitherto seen of Poolvash or Ronaldsway limestone, although there can be little doubt that the materials of the hillock have been transported hither across the limestone areas of the Isle of Man." As a matter of interest, there is also a cap of similar material as that described by Cummings left on Kitterland. The direction of the transportation of all this debris can be determined, because glacial striae can be observed on the Calf running north, north-west to south south-east in the same direction as those on the main island. Many large white quartz boulders are to be seen, not only left on the surface of the land, but also on the shore at low tide. Some of these are of considerable size. There are no reports of any fossils being found.

A number of veins of metal ore exist on the Calf. In 1292 King Edward I granted a licence to John Comyn, the Earl of Buchan, to mine lead to roof the turrets of his castle at Cruggleton in Galloway. The lead ore was probably chipped from exposed seams, and must have been plentiful to have made the work worthwhile. In the 15th, 16th, and 17th centuries the Stanleys prospected for copper. The copper ore was not found to be very plentiful, but it was very rich and produced 6dwt. of copper to every oz. of ore. The possibility of mining was evidently still being considered as late as 1773. In a deed of that date the Duke and Duchess of Athol, leased the Calf to John Quayle and took care to reserve all the mineral rights for themselves. Both lead and copper veins are present at Caigher Point, and J. G. Cumming discovered copper sulphide there in 1846. Miners are of the opinion that the dykes and veins on the Calf, Kitterland, and the point of Aldrick, are related to the lode at Bradda Head on the Isle of Man. The presence of these valuable metals is thought by some to have influenced Thomas Bushell, who was a noted mining engineer, to choose the Calf of Man as his place of hermitage when he lived alone for three years in the 17th century.

There are about 126 acres of once arable and pasture land in the middle of the island. Of these, 28 acres of arable and 61 acres of pasture have been fenced in by the type of dry stone walls so frequently found on the main island. These walls were made in the 18th and early 19th centuries. The areas of old farmlands are, almost exclusively situated over the places where the glacial deposits are found. Some of the fields are situated on each side of the track that leads from the old farmhouse to the lighthouses. Close to the lighthouses are four other small fields which used to be cultivated by the lighthouse keepers and used by them for grazing their cows. Just north of the farmhouse is another small field. However, the bulk of the old farm lands are on the east side of the track which runs from the farm, past the mill, to South Harbour. Unfortunately, as might be expected, the once cultivated land is rapidly becoming overgrown with bracken and heather in spite of the efforts of the wardens and voluntary helpers to keep it clear. The small area to the north-east of Jane's House is now almost completely covered.

On the Calf there are two other areas which were cultivated once and are of a very different kind. These consist of 10 feet wide strips of what used to be called 'Lazy Beds.' These used to be cultivated by scattering corn or setting potatoes on the surface, and then covering the areas with soil taken from trenches at the sides. Some authorities are of the opinion that these sites are prehistoric, but they are more likely to date from Celtic times. It is possible that they are even more recent than that, for this method of cultivation was frequently used for growing potatoes in Ireland. The principal site covers about two acres. It is situated about half a mile north-east of the farmhouse, just south of the road opposite Gibbdale Bay. There is another similar area near South Harbour.

## CHAPTER 2

## THE HERMITS OF THE CALF

It is not at all unusual for a remote area to have a reputation for being a place of refuge for a hermit. The Calf of Man is no exception. It can in fact claim to have had no less than three of them!

Of the first one there is a little evidence, and it is reasonably certain that he did indeed exist, but the existence of the second one is, however, purely Manx folklore. Of the third hermit there is a wealth of written material, although it cannot be called evidence, for it is all based on the word, and the writings of the hermit himself. Most historians, however, having weighed up all the facts of his life, including his acknowledged disappearance from the contemporary scene for the period stated, are of the opinion that his claim to have become a hermit, if only a temporary one, is true.

The first hermit is supposed to have lived on the Calf in the 8th century. He was, it is thought, a Culdee, that is to say one of a fraternity of monks that lived in Ireland and Scotland at that time. The name Culdee has two sources; the first is Old Irish, *cellé dé,* Servants of God or Companions of God; or alternatively the Latinised version *Culdei* which means the same thing. The Culdees usually lived in small groups of cells which were about twelve feet square. They lived a very frugal life and were only allowed a minimum of possessions—a shirt of wool, a cloak to cover it, a jar, a cup for water, and a head covering of some kind. The site of the Culdee's cell on the Calf has never been discovered. As it is known that Christianity first came to the Isle of Man from Ireland, he was in all probability one of the Irish brethren. If he died on the Calf his grave is unknown, as is the reason for his lonely life apart from the rest of his order. It is thought that he built a *Keill* or chapel; although the site of this has become lost there is some little evidence of its existence.

There are three sites for us to consider. The first one has little to recommend it. It is situated at South Harbour and consists of an outline of small stones. It is nineteen feet by eight feet, and is oval in shape, which, to say the least, is unusual. Its only claim to be a *keill* is that its long axis is East/West. The second site is part of what we now call

Bushell's House, situated on the highest part of the island near Oirr Voar, the four-hundred-foot cliff. At the south end of the foundations of this strangely shaped structure is a transept which is of the usual size for a *keill* and which has an East/West orientation. Douglas B. Hague of the Royal Commission on Ancient Monuments in Wales, who visited the island to study the lighthouses, wrote in the Annual Report of the Calf of Man Bird Observatory that he went up to the site to see if it had ever been a coal or turf-burning lighthouse. He exposed some of the foundations of the transept, and came to the conclusion that it was the remains of a *keill*. He was of the opinion that Bushell had cleared the *keill* site and used the area as part of his house. This site has never been properly investigated, so we have no evidence other than that of its orientation and dimensions to substantiate the theory that it was ever a *keill*, or for that matter a house either.

The third site, and the most likely one, is that now occupied by what we call Jane's House, on the northern side of the island, or the nearby plateau. When Jane's House was rebuilt about 1890, four lintel graves were reputed to have been found, and a wall was actually built over two of them. A recent visit failed to reveal any trace of these or the other two, as the area is much overgrown. The presence of these graves would support the theory that the *keill* was in this area. The most important evidence, however, is that of the discovery of the unique Crucifixion Stone which was found somewhere nearby. The widely-held belief that this wonderful work of art was used as the front of an altar would indicate that a *keill* must have been on this site. The presence of the seepage spring providing good water a little way up the hill may also have influenced the Culdee in his choice of area.

Further evidence of the presence of a *keill* on the Calf can be gleaned from old maps. The maps of Speed dated 1605 and 1610, from Durham's Survey of 1595, and the map of Blaeu dated 1645, all bear the symbol for a church or chapel. It should be pointed out, however, that these do not indicate the true position.

There is also some more recent evidence. In the early years of the 20th century, a lady whose father had once farmed the Calf said, "The keill site was a little ledge on the hill slope going up from Cow Harbour to Jane's House. It was then easily to be seen—some big scattered stones in a rough oblong. There were no graves there, they were in a different place altogether." J. R. Bruce, writing in the *Manx Archaeological Survey*, stated that a William Christian of Port Erin had told him in 1931 that his father and mother, who worked on the Calf, used to say that "the little church was in the field in front of the house". At one time it was thought that the farmhouse was meant, but with the other evidence it is obvious that the house to which they referred was Jane's. It is thought that the reason why the graves were found near Jane's House and not on the small plateau, might have been that the soil in the latter area was too shallow.

From the foregoing evidence it is reasonably safe to assume that the Culdee did indeed build a *keill*. It can also be assumed that he was responsible for carving the so called Crucifixion Stone. This could have been brought over in a cargo of stones, but it is rather unlikely as we know that both Jane's House and the farmhouse were built of stones from adjacent quarries. Although there may be doubts about where it was carved, or about who carved it, two facts are certain. Firstly, the Crucifixion Stone was found on the Calf of Man and, secondly, it is a unique example of Celtic art. In 1773 some labourers were working near the site of Jane's House, collecting stones for walling, when one of them noticed the carving of the face of one of the stones. Fortunately he had the wit to appreciate that he had found something unusual, for he put it to one side and showed it to his employer. This was John Quayle, Clerk of the Rolls, who was the tenant of the Calf at that time. John Quayle is reputed to have been an antiquarian by hobby, so he quickly realised the importance of the find.

The Calf of Man Crucifixion Stone is about 25½ inches by 10 inches. It was probably originally about 30 inches high and 15 or 16 inches wide. It is of Manx slate and is carved on one side only. The figure of Christ is completely robed. He has the traditional beard. His arms are out-stretched, and his hands and feet are nailed with very large, round-headed nails. He has a rope girdle, the robe is decorated and bears on the breast what would seem to be a large circular ornament. On the left is the Roman soldier with the spear that was used to pierce Christ's side. This soldier is also bearded and is dressed in Celtic costume! The right side of the stone is missing. In addition to Christ's left arm, it would probably have displayed the soldier with the sponge. J. Romilly Allen in *Early Christian Symbolism in Great Britain and Ireland,* compared the stone with an Irish bronze plaque of the same period, and agreed that the design was Irish Celtic. This way of treating the subject—the robed Christ with the two soldiers—was taken from the earliest attempts to illustrate the Crucifixion in the 6th century in what we now call the Near East. Another authority, Professor Talbot Rice, is of the opinion that the tradition originated in Syria. Some authorities, however, think that the treatment copied by the Irish was Byzantine. It would seem that if the Culdee did indeed carve the stone, he must have copied the design from the cover of his old Gospel book or some other illustration. Professor R. H. Kinvig was of the opinion that the workmanship was finer and more delicate than that of any other stone of the same period.

This unique work of art remained the property of the Quayle family until 1956. It was then bought by the National Art Collection Fund for the sum of £750 and presented to the Manx Museum. The best description of this wonderful discovery is "The Crucifixion Slab" by B. R. S. Megaw, in *The Journal of the Manx Museum, Vol 6.*

The story of the second hermit on the Calf is not so long. It is an old Manx folk story, and is still being told today, especially in the Cregneish area. In the sixteenth century someone killed a woman in a fit of rage and jealousy. There are two stories about this person's origin. Joseph Train in his "History" written in 1845, states that at that time the story concerning the hermit was that he had been: "A person who by his splendour and affluence had been distinguished in the Court of Queen Elizabeth''. The current version is that he was an Irishman and a harpist. Full of remorse, he resolved to lead a solitary life as a penance for his sin. He lived in the old Culdee's cell, or in a cave, on the Calf. On calm evenings the music of his harp could be heard across the Sound. Esther Nelson in her poem ''The Island Penitent'' described his solitary life of remorse.

> "And that old man's harp was of white white bone
> Its strings were soft golden hair
> And the sinner in his sleep would moan
> "Dead! dead! although so fair"
> And the simple islemen many a day
> Held marvel of the same
> And many a mother blessed herself
> For thoughts she might not name.
> And many a maiden's cheek was pale
> To cross the gloomy strath—
> Alas there was a weary curse
> Upon the old man's path."

The third and more recent hermit claimed to have lived a life of solitude on the Calf for three years. Many people have written about his self-imposed exile, but, as mentioned earlier, they have all had to take his word for it; there is no direct proof, only a probability. The name of the third hermit was Thomas Bushell. He was indeed a most remarkable man.

Thomas Bushell was born about 1594 in Broad Marston in Gloucestershire. He was the younger son of Edward Bushell, who was the second son of Sir Edward Bushell of the Manor of Cleve Prior. Thomas Bushell must have been either at odds with his parents or in some kind of trouble, for he left home at the age of fifteen. He entered the service of Sir Francis Bacon, who seems to have been responsible for him going to Balliol College, Oxford. When Bacon became the Lord Chancellor he took Bushell to Court with him. Bushell became something of a dandy, and on one occasion appeared before the King in a splendid coat covered with gold buttons. From this arose the jest common at the time, ''The Chancellor made the buttons, and his man Bushell wore them''. Lord Chancellor Bacon had a great influence on Bushell and did much to educate him, especially upon the subject of minerals, their discovery and mining. Bushell started to speculate heavily in mining ventures, and this resulted in his falling into debt. These debts Bacon paid on several occasions. In 1621 Bacon was accused on twenty-three charges of taking bribes in Chancery suits. He was deprived of his office and imprisoned in the Tower. Bushell himself must have been in danger, for he fled to the Isle of Wight where he lived in the disguise of a fisherman. While there he was accused of being a spy, but managed to clear himself. When things quietened down in England he returned to London.

After Bacon died on April 9th, 1626, Bushell claimed to have become a recluse on the Calf of Man, of which he had learned from Edward Christian, the Governor for the seventh Earl of Derby. Thomas Bushell's own reason for his sojourn on the Calf is contained in his "Mineral Overture to Parliament". "The Embrions of his mines proving abortive by the sudden fall and death of my late Lord Chancellor Bacon in King James' reign, were the motives which persuaded my pensive retirement to a three years unsociable solitude, in ye desolated isle called the Calf of Man, which in obedience to my dead Lord's philosophical advise, I resolved to make a perfect experiment upon myself for the obtaining of a long and healthy life, most necessary for such a repentance as my former debauchedness required, by a parsimonious diet of herbs, oil, mustard, and honey, with water sufficient, most like to yt our long liv'd fathers before the Flood, as was conceived by yt Lord, which I most strictly observed as if obliged by a religious vow, till Divine Pr. called me to a more active life." In the "First Part of Youth's Errors" which Bushell claims was written during his sojourn on the Calf, he wrote "which reduced me to apply for experiment this solitary course to prohibite mee from former follies, and prevent future perils". He had left "an evil bewitching Court to go into a delightful solitarie cave, where no fraud, pride nor deceit inhabits" . . . "God will have my supplications from a poore cell as did Jonas in the whale's belly". Bushell's account of his sojourn on the Calf was widely believed by his contemporaries. There are several writings to prove this. The Reverend Richard James wrote a poem in 1636, seven years after Bushell claimed to have returned from the Calf.

ITER LANCASTRENSE

"If any Bushell will
live West the world withoute projectinge skill
of Ermitage he shall not neede to seeke
in rocks, or Calf of Man an ember weeke."

William Blundell in *A History of the Isle of Man* written in 1648, also mentions Bushell in his chapter on "The Commodities of the Isle of Man". "I make no doubt but ye sea coal, Vitriol, and Alum, might as well be found there (if sought) as well as in Wales, and if Mr. Thomas Bushell's melancholy would have permitted him to have left the Calf to have surveyed the Man itself, he would have found more hopeful encouragement there than since he hath yet found." Later in his book he also refers to Bushell. "All my being in Man they told me there was but one house in all the island (the Calf) and only 2 or 3 servants yt did live on it, it is environed with rocks and there is but one entrance into it. It is not two full miles in compass and is now in the possession of the Earl of Derby, formerly it was the inheritance of the Stevensons of Balladowle". ·He goes on to say "All Man much glorieth in its Calf and do still retain the memory of that vast wit for inventions Mr. Thos. Bushell, where he late had a hermitical life in ye cave in a hollow rock in this island, and do still talk of his pendant bed (such as the hammocks in ships) and strange diet. He built himself a hut on the very summit of the island at a height of 470 feet above the sea and on the verge of an almost perpendicular precipice. It consists of a single room with a narrow entrance to it, and at one side a recess of about three feet wide and six feet deep, probably intended to contain a bed. The ruins of this hut exist to the present day.'' We must remember that this book by Blundell was written in 1648 only nineteen years after Bushell was supposed to have left the Calf. It is obvious that Blundell had no doubts about the story, and his reference to conversations with Manx people about Bushell is corroborative evidence. There was, however, at least one sceptic for a contemporary of Bushell did say "Bushell has told so many improbable stories of his master, and so many silly ones of himself, that he is not to be believed''!

Upon leaving the Calf in 1629 Bushell retired to his property at Road Enstone in Oxfordshire. He again approached Charles I who granted him a licence to manufacture soap by a special method, a skill that he had acquired in addition to that of silk farmer and dyer which he already possessed. In 1637 Charles allowed him to start a Mint in Aberystwyth Castle of sufficient size to deal with all the silver mined in Wales. Bushell then restored the mines previously worked by Sir Hugh Middleton, and drained them by a new method. It took him several years to do this in spite of the employment of a large number of workers. His coins are dated 1638-1642, and are reputed to be some of the most ugly coins ever minted! The mint was then in turn moved to Shrewsbury and Oxford. Bushell repaid the King's generosity by raising a regiment of miners in his support. Thomas Fuller wrote "He converted the mattocks of his miners into spears, and their shovels into shields; formed them into a regiment and lead them in person, in a cause too desperate for recovery''. However, Charles wrote to him in thanks and referred to "Many true services actually done in these times of trying a subject's loyalty, as in raising us the Derbyshire miners for our lifeguard, at our first entrance to this warr for our owne defence. Supplyinge us at Shrewsbury, and Oxford, with your mint for payment of our armye, you charging the dollar wee paid our soldiers at 6/- a piece, when the malignant partie cried them down at five. You stopping the mutinie at Shropshire. You providing us 100 tonnes of lead shot for our armye with mony. You helping us with 26 pieces of ordinance. You clothing our lifeguard and three regiments more with suites, stockings, shoes, and mounterees, when we were readie to march in the ffield. You contratinge with merchants beyond the seas, for providing good quantities of powder, pistol, carbine, muskett, and bullen, in exchange for your own commodities with diverse other services''.

Bushell held the island of Lundy in the King's name up to 1647 when he was forced to surrender it. Bushell, ever an opportunist, then petitioned the Council of State, promising them loyalty in return for a new lease of the Mint. Cromwell granted this and also licensed the Mint.

Bushell's many speculations ultimately led to his downfall, and he finished up in debt. He sent a petition to Charles II, seeking his protection from arrest for a period of two years. In this he mentioned the assistance he had rendered to the King's late father in the past.

Bushell died in 1674 at the age of eighty. He made a nuncupative will. "Wee whose names are hereunder written having been several tymes to visitt Mr. Thomas Bushell in his sickness, often heard him express himself with full resollution, to make the Honourable Colonell Thomas Cullpeper of St Stephen in the County of Kent his Executor, and immediately before he departed this lyfe, being in perfect memory, did, on the One and Twentyth of Aprill present, declare and constitute the said Thomas Cullpeper his sole executor to his last will and testempt. In witness hereof Wee have hereunto set our hands this Two and Twentyth of April 1674. Thomas Coppingor, John Lord, Anthony Winter, The Mark of Mary James." Thomas Bushell is buried in the Cloisters of Westminster Abbey, although his grave is unmarked. A Colonel Chester, who seems to have been the archivist of the Abbey, wrote in 1869, "His burial is not recorded in the official register of Westminster Abbey, which is, I am sorry to say, very imperfect at that period, and I had some doubt about the fact, inasmuch as some authorities say he was buried at Lambeth, but in an old note book of one of the Minor Canons (which we have recently unearthed among the rubbish in the library of the Abbey) and which I accept as authoritative, "Coll. Bushell in the Cloisters 24 April 1674".

This then ends a short biography of this remarkable man, in turn Courtier, Hermit, Silk dyer, Soap maker, Mining engineer, Mint master, Soldier, Author, and Debtor. On the Calf there are two structures bearing Bushell's name. One is known as Bushell's House, in Manx *Thie Vushell*. Cruciform in shape, it is situated on the highest point of the island and consists of stone foundations with some large upright stones. Its long axis is north and south and is roughly 55 feet in length. The transept is about 15 feet by 9 feet. The interior width of the north to south portion is 5 feet three inches, the walls have been two feet thick. On the east side, a little north of the transept, there is a narrow entrance. Between the entrance and the transept is a small stone outhouse 5 feet by 4 feet which is a later addition. Many theories have been advanced about the use of this strange building. The transept is thought by some to have been originally a *keill*. A look-out place is another feasible explanation because of its position. If Bushell did actually build it as a house, he must have had a peculiar taste in architecture, and no thought for his comfort as it is built on the most exposed place on the island, 421 feet high! It must also be noted that in his writing he stated that he lived in a "delightful solitarie cave".

Another place that bears his name is situated on a large rock just separated from the Calf and due south of it. This rock is called the Burroo. On it is a strangely shaped hollow. George Wood in his *Account of the Isle of Man* dated 1811, described it as being then "An excavation of the rock in the form of a cross, each of the two longitudinal cavities being about six feet long, three feet wide, and two feet deep. Immediately at the edge of the cavities is a wall of stone and mortar, two feet high except at the southern, western and eastern ends, which were left open, perhaps for ingress egress, observation and the admission of light. The whole is covered with slate and mortar. Salt water is often to be found in the bottom, in consequence of the sea breaking over the rock in stormy weather, and the stone being too solid to admit of its passage.'' It is called either 'Bushell's Cave' or erroneously 'Bushell's Grave'. We know that Bushell was not buried there. Here again its original use is unknown. It might have been used as a hiding place for silver bullion brought over by Bushell or it may have been some kind of fortification. In spite of its name, it in no way resembles a cave, and one cannot see how Bushell could have lived there. Like 'Bushell's House', it remains a mystery that may never be solved.

# CHAPTER 3
### suggested as a
## PRISONER OF WAR CAMP

It is well known that the Isle of Man was used in both the 1914-18 and the 1939-45 wars as a camp for prisoners of war and detainees of all kinds,but it is less well known that the Calf of Man was once seriously considered for this purpose. This was in 1798 during the war with the French.

It was originally the idea of a Captain S. Gably who had given a great deal of thought to it. He wrote to the Duke of Athol on January 29th, 1798, and set out what were, to his mind, the great advantages in using this unique site. "I. The Calf is remote from the countries that we are or may be at war with. II. It is insulated(isolated?). III. It has good water. IV. Its shores are rocky and difficult to approach except in good weather, and then, on only one small landing place which might be easily guarded. V. The island did not contain any materials that could be used to aid an attempt to escape. VI. France was over 300 miles away. VII.If two or three prisoners were to escape to the Isle of Man, "the well-known timidity of the Manx people would ensure their recapture." VIII. There is plenty of stone on the island from which to build huts—the plainer the better! IX. The Manx Fencibles could be used as guards."

He suggested that a very small naval force cruising around the island in fine weather would prevent escapes, and that if the weather were bad no escape would be possible.

On reading this long and detailed letter from Captain Gably, one cannot help thinking that he was in no small measure activated by self-interest, for he concludes his letter by saying that if the suggestion was favourably considered he would do all that he could to help, as he had to retire from the army!

Captain Gably must have received a certain amount of encouragement from the Duke, for he then visited the Calf (no small effort in those days) and made a personal inspection of the facilities. He wrote again to the Duke on March 9th, 1798, and reported that the water supply was excellent as there were "three small rills that never failed." Heather and

Jane's House and the Sound, looking towards Port Erin on the Isle of Man.

Ling were very plentiful, the former would make good bedding and the latter excellent fuel. He had probably seen Ling used as fuel on the main island, for it was frequently burned on the *Chiollagh* or fire stone in the cottages at that period. "Turf for fuel was also plentyful."

He went on to suggest that a very small force could easily guard 20,000 prisoners, and that Peel smacks or revenue cutters could be used as guard ships. He reminded the Duke that at the present time there were no less than 2,000 prisoners of war in the Liverpool gaols alone; these could be sent over and the gaol refilled. The problem of building the houses could be overcome, as no doubt there would be many stone-masons among the prisoners. In the meanwhile they could camp. He concluded hopefully that if the Lords of the Admiralty felt like sending someone for further observation, his services were available!

The Duke then consulted Governor Shaw for *his* observations on the subject. The Governor wrote to the Duke on March 10th, 1798. He agreed that the Calf could be made suitable, and also stressed the advantages of the high cliffs and strong currents. He strongly urged the duke to appoint someone he knew, or could trust, as a Naval Commander. The Governor seemed to have a very small opinion of the local Manx gentry, for he went on to say that "there was no one on the Island that he could vouch for, they might make the service subservient to their own interest or convenience"! As so often happens in these cases, poor retired Captain Gably, having served his purpose, was dropped and is heard of no more.

The Duke seems to have been quite keen on the plan, probably because he had much to gain as he owned the Calf. He wrote to the Secretay of State for War on March 31st, 1798, and suggested that if the authorities thought that the Calf might be suitable for the purpose, they should send someone to report on its feasibility.

However, Governor Shaw seems to have had second thoughts on the matter, and had become quite perturbed by the rumours that he had heard, for on May 4th, 1798, he again wrote to the Duke expressing his unease; "there is a kind cf terror mixed with some murmurings going forth among the people . . . at the very idea of prisoners being sent here". He also stressed the difficulty in guarding them. He was glad to report that he had not actually heard any criticism, although of course he realized that one of the Duke's interests would be to raise the revenue from the Calf.

It would seem that someone was appointed to examine the matter thoroughly, for there is a report from an E. Fisher dated May 11th, 1798, addressed to the Hon. Commissioners. His principal objection was that he thought that the Irish might help the French to escape, and to combat that suggested "A formidable military guard". "Two armed cutters mounting 12 guns each, and six small vessels of about 26 tons, would be sufficient to keep off any Irish wherrys, or other small vessels that might be used."

He thought that a rescue attempt might be made in the herring season, when there were many boats in the vicinity.

His other objections were, that all the provisions for the prisoners would have to be imported from either Northern Ireland or Liverpool, except for fish and potatoes. Beer, however, could be brewed on the Isle of Man. Three months' provisions must be kept in stock on the Calf at all times, as it is frequently inaccessible. It would take at least two seasons to accommodate 10,000 men.

The Duke, like Captain Gably before him, was thwarted in his ambitions, for that was the last that was heard of the matter!

# CHAPTER 4

## FOLKLORE

As the Celtic people were renowned story tellers, and the Norse famous for their sagas, one would expect that the Manx, who are descended from a combination of both, would have a rich tradition of folklore; and this of course is the case. In the days when common folk could neither read nor write, these stories were circulated and told when sitting before the fire. The stories were called *Skeealyn* in Manx.

Many of these tales were carried as a kind of stock-in-trade by the itinerant craftsmen who roamed the Isle of Man selling their services as tinkers, woodworkers, or tailors, spending a night or two at each farm before moving on. Many of the farms actually set aside small buildings specially to accommodate these people and the ubiquitous beggars. It was, of course, a great pleasure for the family to be regaled with a story or two during the long winter evenings.

"Southwest of the Calf there is a large sandbank. It lies under forty fathoms of water, but at one time it was an island well above the sea. It was the home of Mannanan Mac-y-Lear who was the Chief of a race of three-legged giants. These giants used to raid the Calf and carry off cattle and maidens. If they were pursued they would row or sail back to their island, which they would hide away by magic in a bank of fog."

Mannanan-Beg-Mac-y-Leirr, to give him another name, was reputed to be not only a King but a Warrior, Trader, Magician, and Navigator. He also appears in Welsh and Irish folk tales.

Another version of the same story says that "The old people used to say that there was a strange enchanted island south-west of the Calf. It was only seen once in seven years when Old May Day was on a Sunday. Some feller by the name of Onny Vadrill was the last one that saw it, but it is often cloudy in May, and the people used to be up looking for it for many years."

A story about the Sound tells that "Some years ago there were two men fishing near the Calf, and they saw a little dog on a rock near the water. It was as pretty a little thing as they ever met, and they went to get it. One went on shore, and he was just in the act of taking hold of the

The farmhouse, now the Bird Observatory, with its range of outbuildings.

dog when it disappeared in a flash of fire, and both men were sick for a long time afterwards."

George Wood tells the following story in his book *An Account of the Past and Present State of the Isle of Man,* written in 1811. "While waiting at Port Erin for the departure of a herring boat that was to convey me to the Calf, a fisherman introduced himself by warning me to take care of the fairies which I should meet with there, telling me that he had a charm against their power. Another fisherman who that morning had walked near two miles out of his way to show me the road, pretended to laugh at his companion's tales . . . . but he said that his father had once met a flock of them, and he was not a man to tell a lie. 'They were invisible, but cackled like geese close to him when there were no geese within sight'."

Another folk tale concerning the Sound claims that ". . . there is a large cave that can be entered by boat. Its name is *Giau Kione Dhoo,* or Black Head Creek. A long time ago it was a storehouse used by a cruel pirate. When the pirate sailed away on one of his raids, he used to leave one of his men behind in the cave to guard the treasure that he kept there. One day the pirate and his crew sailed away to attack some ships, and he never came back again. The guard on the cave waited for many years until he became an old man and died. Several years later, an old Manx fisherman was fishing in the Sound and he was surprised to see a boat rowed by six men in red caps enter the cave. Being of a curious nature he also rowed in through the only entrance. He looked around, but the cave was completely empty. The boat and the six men had vanished."

Kitterland, the islet in the Sound, is much larger than it would seem when viewed from a small boat at sea level. It has about an acre of pasture on it. The late Thomas Clague used to place lambs on Kitterland in the Spring, and leave them there to fatten. Because of legal difficulties it was not possible to trace the ownership of Kitterland in olden times. However, it is doubtful if it had the same owner as the Calf. It is more likely that it was linked with land on the Isle of Man. About the year 1900 Thomas Clague bought Kitterland and some farmland on the main island near the Sound, in partnership with a Mr. Harry Maddrell of Ballamaddrell. They eventually sold the farmland but each retained a half share in Kitterland.

Kitterland is supposed to have received its name from that of a famous Viking Chief in King Olaf's day, who was called Kitter. There is an interesting story to explain this. Kitter was reputed to be a mighty hunter. Over the years he had succeeded in slaughtering all the wild life in the south of the Isle of Man. One day he was told that the Calf of Man contained some splendid Red Deer, so he left his house on South Barrule with a party of men to hunt them. When the Celtic people who lived in the south of the Isle of Man heard this, they were determined to get rid of him if at all possible. They feared that once he had finished off the last of the deer in the area, he would turn his attention to their cattle and slay them. They thought that if Kitter lost his house, he would go away and leave them and the animals in peace. So by means of witch-craft they set fire to it. Kitter's cook had been left behind to guard the house. His name was Eaoch which meant "someone who can cry out loud". On seeing the house on fire the cook let out such a mighty shout that Kitter, hunting on the Calf, was able to hear it. He immediately gathered his men together, and they hastened down to the Sound and embarked in their coracle. Unfortunately, during their hunt the tide had changed and the Sound was in its most dangerous condition. The coracle was smashed onto what we now call Kitterland, and he and his men were drowned.

# CHAPTER 5

## THE LIGHTHOUSES

### PHAROS LOQUITUR

Far in the bosom of the deep
O'er these wild shelves my watch I keep
A ruddy gem of changeful light
Bound on the dusky brow of night
The seaman bids my lustre hail
And scorns to strike his timorous sail

Sir Walter Scott.

The earliest reference to lighthouses on the Calf is perhaps the two additions to the map of Richard D. Wilson published in 1771. These show coal-burning lighthouses, one opposite the Burroo and another opposite Bushell's House. The date of these drawings is unknown, nor is it known who built the lighthouses or were responsible for them. They would consist of iron braziers of brightly burning coal. They were usually set on a high site, sometimes on a small tower. If they did indeed exist on the Calf, their light would not be visible from any great distance and would probably only be of assistance to local fishermen.

At the end of the 18th century, the owners of ships which had to sail past the east coast of the Isle of Man were becoming increasingly concerned about their great losses on that dangerous side of the Manx coast. It is interesting to study the correspondence with the Duke of Athol on the subject of erecting a much needed lighthouse on the Calf. This shows the most appalling procrastination over a period of no less than forty-seven years, during which time many ships were lost, for the lack of a light to guide them.

On December 30th, 1771, John Quayle wrote to the Duke and said that a Mr. Ludwidge had taken part of Langness and had proposed to the shipping trade of Whitehaven and Workington, that he was prepared to build a lighthouse there as a private venture, if they would agree to a levy of one penny a ton light money. Many of these ship owners had agreed to this, but the Liverpool owners did not favour Langness at all.

They much preferred the Calf because its great height would make a light more visible. The Liverpool traders were also not in favour of a private venture of this kind, and thought that trustees should be appointed. They suggested that the rent of the necessary land could either be agreed direct or through an arbitrator.

On January 8th, 1772, John Quayle and Dan Mylrea wrote to the Duke, saying that the scheme for a lighthouse on the Calf was supported by the opinion of a Mr. McKenzie, who had undertaken an accurate survey of the whole channel. The writers also felt that no damage would be done to the island, and that the proposed light would be of great benefit to the countryside in general. The Duke replied on January 22nd stating that he agreed that the Calf would be a most suitable site, and that he would refer the rent to the Commissioners if the scheme was carried out.

No less than twenty-five years were allowed to elapse before the next reference to a lighthouse contained in an undated memorandum written about 1797 by a Captain G. Small. In this, he mentions the light again and the advantages to be gained by the merchants of Liverpool, Whitehaven, and Dublin, who would willingly subject their vessels to a "Handsome duty" if it could be effected.

About a year later a Mr. Colquhoun wrote a memorandum for the consideration of the public, to exert their influence in preventing the many heavy calamities resulting in the loss of rich property and valuable lives. He mentioned the attempt of Mr. Ludwidge to have a light put on Langness, and how this was ultimately considered unsuitable as the Calf was a better site. "Since that period, not a year has passed without shipwrecks on the coast from the Calf to Langness, to name those of one year from November 1794, these were to the number of nine." He went on to enumerate these and describe the loss of lives and cargo. He stated how, for the lack of a light, the masters of ships had either to steer wide of the island or lay-to at night if the weather was unsuitable. He stressed the importance of a light on the Calf, as mariners in mid-channel would be able to see both that light and the one on Holyhead. He advocated a double light on the Calf so that mariners would be sure to distinguish it from that on the Skerries. He concluded by expressing surprise that such an important matter should have been neglected for so long, and urged all those concerned to form a committee to look into the question of feasibility and costs.

Little or no notice seems to have been taken of this plea, for another thirteen years were to elapse before the matter was heard of again. On 4th April, 1813, Captain J. Cotton wrote to the Duke informing him that the first step would be for the shipping trade to inform Trinity House of the necessity for a lighthouse, and that "they would be prepared to pay a reasonable sum for its maintenance". He went on to say that the terms of subscription for the Holyhead and Skerries lighthouses would probably be acceptable to the trade. There is a note at the bottom of the letter in another hand, "Holyhead one penny a ton, Skerries ditto".

It now took another two years before anything further was done, for on 2nd May, 1815, the Commissioners of Northern Lights wrote to the Duke. They stated that their attention had been drawn repeatedly by the trade to the great hazard to which their shipping was exposed, for want of lights on the extreme points of the Isle of Man, and that they were prepared to apply for power to remedy the defect. They were of the opinion that no duties were to be levied other than enough to defray their expenses, and that these duties would be small. They had sufficient funds and able engineers to accomplish their objects, and requested His Grace to submit his views on the matter. It would seem that His Grace was in no hurry to submit his views, for it took another two years before at last things started to move in earnest.

On January 15th, 1817, Sir William Rae on behalf of the Commissioners wrote a letter to the Duke in which he queried the amount of compensation to be paid for the required ground, which was usually about ten acres. While under the Act they could have the rents fixed by a Jury, they had never had to resort to that, as until then every proprietor had been most reasonably disposed. They were surprised, therefore, to find that in addition to paying a ground rent, they were expected to pay no less than a further £50 a year, because the tenant of the Calf would no longer have the exclusive right to it. The Commissioners were of the opinion that their proposal to erect a harbour would have added greatly to the convenience of the tenant. They would never consider such an unreasonable demand, and would if necessary resort to Parliament for powers to take the ground at a fair value. They trusted that this would not be necessary, and that His Grace·would use his influence with the tenant.

Two months later, on March 7th, 1817, John Spottiswood of London wrote complaining that the Commissioners had not yet received a reply to their letter, and stating that nothing further could be done until they had. Another three months passed without a reply from the Duke, for on April 26th, 1817, Sir William Rae again wrote to the Duke. He said that he had not received a reply to his letter of January 15th. He went on to say that the trade were complaining about the delay. If anything was to be done this season, work must be commenced immediately. If the Duke's mind was not yet made up, perhaps an arbitrator could be appointed.

The Duke must have at last replied to the Commissioners, for on June 7th, 1817, they wrote accepting his offer of ten acres of land on the Calf, on a yearly quit rent of ten pounds a year, the Duke to satisfy all claims that might be made by the tenant. At last, after no less than forty-seven years of procrastination, during which uncounted vessels were lost and their unfortunate crews drowned, agreement was reached. The Commissioners must have been optimistic about the outcome of their wrangle concerning the rent, and done much preliminary work, for it only took a further ten months to complete the job. At long last on the night of February 1st, 1818, the lights were lit.

In actual fact two lighthouses had to be built, so placed that the line of their lights pointed to the submerged rock off the southern extremity of the island known as Chickens Rock. These lights were 560 feet apart. The lower light was 305 feet above the sea, and the higher light 396 feet above. They carried double revolving lights, visible for six to seven leagues in favourable weather. These lights attained their most luminous effect as they revolved, at the end of each two minutes. Synchronisation was checked by the light-keepers so that at the same instant in each direction the lights were either visible or eclipsed. This characteristic was effective in giving a clear distinction from other lighthouses, but the expense of establishing two adjacent towers, each with a revolving light, could be justifiable only where, as in this instance, an outlying danger must be indicated by special means.

These twin towers were in use until 1875, when a sea tower was constructed on the Chickens Rock. This gets its name from that of the sea birds, the Stormy Petrels, sometimes called Mother Carey's Chickens.

The building of the Chickens Rock lighthouse was commenced in 1869, but it was not until January 1st, 1875, that the light was exhibited for the first time. The granite used for its construction was quarried at Dalbeattie, Kirkcudbrightshire, Scotland, and then shipped to Port St. Mary. There, the stonemasons carefully shaped every block, dovetailing one piece into another. Layer by layer, the lighthouse was built on the land, and layer by layer it was shipped to the Rock. The foundations are 15 feet down into the solid stone. The lower 32 feet 8 inches of the tower, which is 143 feet high, is solid. The wall of the tower weighs 3,557 tons. A tonite fog signal was added in 1890.

On December 23rd, 1960, the interior of the building was partly destroyed by fire. Fire in any situation is a dreadful thing, but the horror of a fire in a lighthouse tower on an isolated rock almost defies description. The three men on the Chickens Rock at the time were the principal, Jack Ross, Leslie Anderson who gave the following account, and Andrew Brown.

The fire was caused by an explosion. The chimney in the kitchen compartment had just been swept and had naturally created a lot of dirt. To speed up the cleaning, one of the keepers used some petrol on a rag. Somehow the petrol vapour became ignited and exploded in the confined space. An attempt was made to put out the fire with extinguishers, but the men, beginning to feel themselves overcome by the smoke, had to abandon the attempt and retreated up the tower, closing the steel hatches of each of the two bedroom compartments behind them until they reached the light room at the top. Their attempt to signal for help by radio failed because the batteries of the set were situated in a compartment below the kitchen level, so the cables had been destroyed by the fire. Rockets were then fired, and these were seen from the Cregneish radio station on the main island. The Port St. Mary lifeboat, which is always kept afloat, was immediately sent to the rescue.

In the meantime the three keepers on the top of the tower, which was by now virtually a chimney, decided to try to reach the comparative safety of the rocks below. Keeper Anderson managed to lower the other two by means of a rope, but unfortunately on attempting to slide down himself, found the he could not control his speed of descent, and the friction badly burned both hands. They then decided to re-enter the tower through the door in the base, only to find that burning debris from above was falling onto the oil tanks in the basement room. They managed to put this fire out with buckets of sea water. During this time, the principal keeper Jack Ross badly burned both arms through coming into contact with a steel ladder which was almost red hot.

When the lifeboat arrived it was realised that the only way to take the men off would be by means of a Breeches Buoy, and an attempt was first made to take off Anderson. This proved to be very difficult as the movement of the boat prevented the lines being kept taut, and Anderson spent as much time under the sea as above it! As the other two keepers were comparatively safe in the doorway, the Port St. Mary boat took Anderson to Port Erin, where by now the lifeboat there had been launched. The two boats now went together to the Chickens Rock, and with some difficulty managed to rescue the other two keepers.

Although after an inspection it was found that the damage to the lighthouse was principally confined to the kitchen, because of the keepers' precautions in closing the various compartments' steel doors, it was realised that the amount of work required to bring the lighthouse up to modern standards would prove to be too costly. The Board had had experience of this after a fire in the Skerryvore lighthouse. As a consequence, it was decided to convert the light to an unattended one; so on September 20th, 1962, after extensive repairs, a permanent unwatched propane-gas light was established 125 feet above the sea.

The intensity of the light is now only 4,600 candelas (previously 173,000 candelas) with a range of thirteen miles. A permanent unwatched electric foghorn was established in November 1968.

When manned, four lightkeepers, three of them doing duty at the one time, were attached to the Chickens Rock, and they carried out duties on a rotation basis—four weeks on the rock, followed by two weeks ashore. Their wives and families resided at a shore station at Port St. Mary. From there the attending boat made the fortnightly relief trips when weather permitted. The automatic light is now maintained by an Attendant Keeper who also lives at Port St. Mary.

After the conversion of the Chickens lighthouse, the Northern Lighthouse Board decided to build a new lighthouse, once again on the Calf itself. Owing to the difficulties of access to the site, all the materials for building were flown to the island by helicopter, some 870 tons being lifted from Port St. Mary or Cregneish to a small plateau near the site. The landing place was outlined by white quartz glacier-borne boulders. It is interesting to wonder what archaeologists will make of this white circle if it is excavated in a thousand years from now. They will probably think it was the site of some strange religious ceremony!

The new light is situated 312 feet above sea level, with a maximum of over two million candlepower; it will be visible for twenty-three miles in clear weather. It is also equipped with a powerful fog signal, operated by compressed air. The plan of the buildings is very different from that of the old ones. They form three sides of a hollow square, with a squat light tower at one corner.

The accommodation for the four lightkeepers is of the most modern design, and there is internal access to the engineroom, light tower, and watchroom. The system of staff rotation is the same as that for the old Chickens Rock light. The new lighthouse is in constant radio communication with the light on Langness, where connection can be made with the public telephone system. The lightkeepers are much more free on the Calf than they were on the Chickens. Not only do they have a garden, but they have even constructed a small golf course!

# CHAPTER 6

## WRECKS

During the days of sail, wrecks were common round the wild coasts of the Isle of Man, and the number of vessels lost seems to be almost unbelievable today. In one year, from November, 1794, no less than nine ships, some of which were a considerable size, were wrecked between the Calf and Langness. In the twenty-five years between 1821 and 1846, 144 ships were lost around the Manx coasts and 172 men were drowned. Some of the boats were, of course, only small, Schooners, Luggers, and Smacks being the most common.

The Calf has had its share of these calamities, for of the 144 it is possible to identify seven wrecked on or in the immediate vicinity of the island. One of the larger ships is mentioned later; the details of the six smaller ones are as follows.

1823.   The Smack *Emilia* of Port St. Mary, is supposed to have struck the Calf, for she was lost with all hands. There was a crew of 8.

1824.   The Smack *Peel Castle* of Peel, was lost with her crew of 6 in a similar way.

1827.   The Brig *Lion* of Workington, foundered close to the Calf.

1828.   The Schooner *George* of Derbyhaven struck the Calf and was lost.

1839.   The Lugger *Victoria* of Peel, aground on the Calf, became a total loss.

1840.   The Schooner *Anna Sophia* of Yarmouth foundered close in to the Calf.

Some of the wrecks on or near the Calf were caused by the dearth of lighthouses in earlier days. Some ships lost their sails, or became dismasted in a gale, while others during foggy conditions were drawn into the Sound by the powerful and relentless tidal current. Even powerful modern steamships were not immune from this disaster as will be seen later.

The one large sailing vessel previously mentioned was wrecked in the Goll-ny-Varroo. She was the *Young Halliday* of Liverpool, whose Master was C. Byrne. Laden with a cargo of raw cotton bales, she sailed from Savannah bound for Greenock. On March 8th, 1821, she became lost in a dense fog, and in spite of the two new lighthouses erected on the Calf only three years previously, she ran aground at 3 a.m. Fortunately the sea was calm, so the crew were able to save themselves with some difficulty; they probably scrambled over the rocks on to the Calf.

Unfortunately the Master had to report that the well-known rapidity and danger of the current at this point made the salvage of the badly-holed vessel very doubtful. The next day he was chagrined to see the greater part of his cargo being carried away westward by the tide as the bales floated out of the hold.

He also placed on record his appreciation of the great kindness shown by Mr. Dawson, the tenant of the Calf, who did all that he could for the comfort of his exhausted crew.

Apart from minor losses, there have been three vessels of considerable size wrecked in the Sound. The first large wreck that is known is a Russian ship of 700 tons in 1786. No details of this wreck are available, except that all her unfortunate crew were lost, and that some of the ship's rats were able to swim to the Calf and infest the island which up to then had been free of those vermin.

The next wreck provides a most interesting and somewhat macabre story. This disaster occurred to the 160-ton Brigantine *Lily* of Liverpool on 28th December, 1852. A Brigantine, usually shortened to Brig, is a two-masted square-rigged vessel. The wreck happened during a south-west gale of almost hurricane force. During the day several sailing vessels were seen from the Isle of Man, partially dismasted and running before the wind. A number of large pieces of wreckage were washed up on the Manx coast, including an empty lifeboat from the *British Queen* that came ashore in Castletown Bay.

The *Lily* was loaded with fire-arms, cannon, cotton goods, rum, general cargo and sixty tons of gunpowder. She carried a crew of thirteen, and was bound for Ambriz on the west coast of Africa. As she sailed to pass the south of the Isle of Man in the gale, having been driven back from Cork, she lost some of her sails and was relentlessly driven into the Sound by the wind and tide. The Captain ordered one of the anchors to be dropped, but by some mischance it was not properly shackled to the cable and so was lost. An attempt was then made to drop the second anchor which was carried on the deck, but this became hung up on an obstruction and would not fall. The helmsman, seeing what he thought to be a fairly wide channel between the main island and the Calf, attempted to steer through, but, as was inevitable under those conditions, the Brig smashed aground onto a rock adjacent to Kitterland. The shock of impact brought down one of the masts which fell on the ship's carpenter, killing him instantly. The ship's deck was then swept by a wave which washed some of the crew overboard to their deaths.

The Captain and six members of the crew managed to leave the ship which they expected to slide back into deep water, by scrambling over the bows onto the rock that they had struck. The Captain, seeing the comparative safety of Kitterland so near, foolishly attempted to swim across but was washed away and drowned. The remaining crew members were all ultimately rescued and taken to Port St. Mary. They were all in remarkably good condition in spite of their ordeal, except one who unfortunately had to have a leg amputated. The loss of the Captain and the other six crew members was, however, nothing compared to the disaster that was to follow.

On the following day the wreck was reported to a Mr. Lace. He was at that time the Manx sub-agent for Lloyds, who carried the insurance on the vessel and cargo. Lace went down to see the *Lily* which was still reasonably intact, but he was concerned to see that some of the cargo, for which he was now responsible, was being washed ashore onto the main island and was being pilfered by the spectators. He returned to Castletown and asked the police to protect it; he also gathered together a party of twenty-seven men to help with the salvage. These men, together with the police, headed by the Chief Constable, went down to the Sound. A rough gangway was laid across the rocks to the *Lily,* which was by now high and dry, and most of the men boarded the ship. They quickly noticed smoke coming from one of the hatch covers, so while some men formed a bucket chain, the carpenter cut a hole in the deck in order to pour the water through into the hold. As soon as the axe pierced the deck the gunpowder blew up. The explosion was both heard and felt twenty miles away, and a piece of the *Lily* was ultimately found in the Mill field on the outskirts of Castletown. Houses were shaken in Douglas, and miners working in Ballacorkish Mine three miles away felt the shock underground. Their candles were extinguished and one man was knocked off his feet. They were so frightened that they left the mine and came up to the surface.

Twenty-five of the men who were on board, including Lace and two of the constables, were blown to pieces and not a vestige of these men was ever seen again. Some other men who were on Kitterland were killed but were capable of identification. The only survivor was James Kelly. He was standing on the gangway with a bucket of water when the ship blew up, and was hurled some distance onto the rocks. When he regained consciousness, although badly injured he endeavoured to bathe his face in the water of a rock pool, only to find it full of blood! Pieces of the victims, together with the shattered remnants of the rest of the cargo, were afterwards found scattered on the whole area around the Sound and even on the Calf. The explosion would have been even more severe but for the fact that when the *Lily* struck, a large amount of gunpowder was washed out of the hold. Many quarter-casks of this were eventually washed up at Port Erin.

The Governor and the High Bailiff launched an appeal for funds to assist the twenty-two widows and seventy-four orphans who were left. A large meeting was addressed by the Rev. R. Dixon, D.D., the Principal

Top: The disused upper lighthouse. (1818).
Bottom: The ruined mill and millstone.

of King William's College. Unfortunately some of the money subscribed was lost in the financial crash of a local bank.

Many years later, a man dying in America made a confession that he was partly responsible for the tragedy. He stated that in the early hours of the morning he, together with two companions, boarded the *Lily* with the object of plundering her. As it was dark in the hold they had lit a candle, and on leaving the vessel they had left the candle still alight inside. It is thought that the candle ignited some of the cotton goods which continued to smoulder. When the carpenter pierced the deck with his axe the fire flared up, detonating the gunpowder.

The remains of the men were interred in Rushen churchyard, and a stone of Pooilvaaish black marble bears the names of those lost.

In 1858 another sailing vessel was lost in the Sound. She was a French ship, the *Jeanne St. Charles.* Finding himself close to Spanish Head in a gale, the Captain in his ignorance foolishly tried to anchor and was caught in the notorious current as the tide rose. The anchors dragged, being quite unable to hold the ship which drifted very gradually into the Sound. Her desperate plight was seen from Spanish Head, and the news of the impending disaster was taken to Port St. Mary. There, two boats were manned by volunteers who went to her aid. Although there seemed to be little that they could do for the ship, they thought that they might have been able to take off the crew. When the Captain realised that the vessel was doomed he ordered the ship's boat to be lowered and the crew scrambled on board. However, in spite of all their efforts, the small boat became caught in the same current and drifted with the ship until both ship and boat struck Thousla at the western end of the Sound. The crew, which included two ship's boys, clung onto the rock until the Port St. Mary boats arrived. The boats took two hours to reach the Sound from Port St. Mary, and in moderating conditions managed to take the men off. Unfortunately the two boys, exhausted by the wet and cold, were not strong enough to cling on to Thousla and so were swept off and drowned.

The Port St. Mary men quickly realised that they would not be able to return to their own village against the wind, and wisely decided to carry on, landing at Port Erin. This tragic event of 116 years ago is marked to this day, for the Commissioners of Northern Lights erected a concrete tower surmounted by an iron cross to mark the position of Thousla and to provide something to cling to should a similar event ever happen again.

The next wreck in the Sound was of a very different kind of vessel. She was the *Clan McMaster,* a cargo boat of 6,563 tons. She was wrecked on September 30th, 1923. The *Clan McMaster* was a well-found vessel and of quite a large size for that period. She had loaded part of her cargo at Glasgow and was proceeding to Liverpool to load the remainder. The cargo which was taken on in Scotland consisted of heavy and light machinery, sewing machines, cotton goods, and 2,000 tons of coal. She was ultimately bound for Eastern ports.

On the night of the 30th the whole of the area around the Isle of

Man was covered by a dense fog and the Captain, who for some reason could not get a bearing from the Chickens Rock lighthouse, thought that he was six miles from the Calf. There were no radio beacons or radar in those days. He thought that under the circumstances it would be prudent to reduce his speed to dead slow—just enough to provide steerage way. Little did he know that he was just off the north of the Sound. As soon as she slowed, the *Clan McMaster,* unknown to the Captain, was caught in the full force of the notorious current and she was driven onto the rocks in what is known as The Blind Sound. This is an area between Thousla and the Calf. The time was 1.30 a.m. on Sunday. An S.O.S. was promptly sent out, and this was picked up at Liverpool. The crew of the *Clan McMaster* numbered eighty; fifty-four of these were coolies, or Lascars as they were sometimes called. They all managed to reach the Calf in safety and eventually took refuge in Jane's House.

Crowds of local people went to see the wreck during the afternoon of the same day. At that time she was only down a little at the stern, smoke was still coming from the funnel, and the ropes were hanging from some of the davits although it is understood the boats were not used.

The next day the officers returned to the ship, and rumour had it that the local lads had already been on board and taken much movable property including the Captain's binoculars! They are even supposed to have unbolted the brass Ship's binnacle, but this story is probably apocryphal. The Lascar crew refused to re-board the ship, but the officers managed to get the pumps working. They were wasting their time, however, for the double bottom of the ship had been pierced by the rock. The newly-risen seas were also already swinging the vessel round by the stern, which had now started to settle ever deeper into the water.

The Liverpool salvage ship *Ranger* came over, and being small was able to tie up alongside. As it was by now too rough for a motor or rowing boat to land on the Calf, the Lascars were taken off by breeches buoy. The crew had fared quite well for food, for among other things they had taken the carcass of a sheep to the Calf that they had slaughtered immediately before leaving the stricken vessel. The coolies in those days always carried live sheep with them when at sea. They also took their precious ram ashore with them alive. The *Ranger* managed to salvage some of the light goods from the forehold. The sea had already submerged all of the ship aft of the midships engineroom.

The *Clan McMaster* was worth about £100,000 and the cargo a similar sum, which was a very large amount in those days. The ship, of course, became a total loss. It was astonishing to see the result of the terrific action of the seas in the Sound. Within a month or so practically nothing was left, and in less than a year the *Clan McMaster* had completely disappeared.

One cannot describe the next event as a wreck because the vessel was eventually saved. The story, however, does illustrate that even in modern times, in spite of all the latest aids to navigation, ships are at risk from the relentless current that sets in towards the Sound at the change of the tide.

On the morning of Wednesday July 9th, 1958, Lieutenant-Commander Frank Williams, who was at that time the Warden on the Calf, came out of the farmhouse to make his way down to the Sound. The Calf, with the Isle of Man, had been covered with a thick blanket of mist all night, and although it was now daylight he could hardly see his way along the track. Suddenly he saw looming out of the mist two men walking in the opposite direction, on what he thought was an uninhabited island. They told him that they were Angus Campbell and Donald McNeill, the mate and a seaman from the Scottish Coaster *St. Ronan,* that had run aground near the north end of the Sound. The *St. Ronan,* which belonged to J. A. Gardner and Company of Glasgow, was on her maiden voyage from Koping in Sweden to Runcorn, Cheshire, with a cargo of 600 tons of felspar. During the dense mist of the night before, the Captain had thought that he was well clear of the Isle of Man, but had nevertheless rung down to the engineroom for 'Dead Slow' as a precaution. Unknown to him he was much closer to the island than he thought, and his action of reducing speed had exactly the same effect on the *St. Ronan* as it had had on the ill-fated *Clan McMaster* thirty-five years earlier. The *St. Ronan* swept on to disaster without the Captain's knowledge as she was caught in the tremendous current which was created as the tide rushed through the Sound. This happened at 4 a.m., when with a tremendous crash the Coaster was smashed onto the rocks. The unfortunate Captain thought that he was aground on the Isle of Man, and tried to establish radio contact to summon assistance, only to find that his transmitter had been put out of action as a result of the collision with the rocks. The only thing that he could do was to wait for daylight or for the mist to clear. He had a thorough check made, and as the vessel seemed to be well aground and was making very little water, he came to the conclusion that she was safe for the time being. As soon as there was enough light, Campbell and McNeill offered to scramble over the rocks and climb up onto the land to try and make contact with someone. They eventually found the track and were following it when they almost collided with Williams.

The Captain of the *St. Ronan* could not have chosen a more suitable place to run aground for, by a strange coincidence, not only did the Calf have a new radio telephone but also a fully qualified salvage officer in the person of the Warden, who had spent the last four years of his Naval service in just that capacity. Williams promptly contacted the Douglas police, told them what had happened, and asked them to summon assistance; he then went down to the ship to see what he could do to help. After inspecting the vessel, which he found to have the bow section high on the rocks in two fathoms of water, he went down into the ship and was pleased to find her reasonably watertight.

His advice to the Captain was to pump the fuel oil from the forward tank into the tanks at the stern. He also suggested that they lay out a kedge anchor from the stern and await the next high tide. When that time arrived the engines should be run astern and the windlass draw on the anchor. In the meantime the Port Erin lifeboat arrived in response to Williams' message to the police, having left Port Erin at 6.30 a.m. The lifeboat established radio contact with Portpatrick radio station and sent off a "no immediate danger" signal. The message was relayed to Lloyds of London who had insured the vessel and cargo. Lloyds as a precaution arranged for tugs to be sent from Cobh, and also sent their Manx representative to the scene. Fourteen hours after the *St. Ronan* struck the rocks, when the tide was once again at its maximum, the engines were run "full astern" and the windlass drew on the kedge anchor. The result surprised every one, including the unfortunate Captain. The Coaster slid off the rocks with so much way on that she fouled the anchor cable and wound it around the propeller! After further small mishaps all was eventually put right, and the vessel resumed her eventful maiden voyage under her own steam. The tugs were then signalled to return as their expensive services were no longer required. The *St. Ronan* proved to be an unlucky ship, for after going into dry dock for inspection and repair, she set sail again and only eight weeks after running aground on the Calf, she ran onto the Goodwin Sands and this time became a total loss.

CHAPTER 7

## THE HISTORY OF THE MANX SHEARWATER
## (PUFFINUS PUFFINUS)

No book on the Calf would be complete without a chapter about the interesting Manx Shearwater, the only bird to bear a Manx name. The Manx Shearwater was intimately associated with the Calf and at one time nested there in tens of thousands. It was sometimes called the "Manks Puffin" and it did not receive its present name until 1676.

The earliest reference to this enormous colony of sea-birds occurs in one of the Norse sagas, that of Njal. In it he tells a strange story of two Viking Chiefs, Brodir and Ospak. In the early part of the year 1014, Ospak had over 100 ships lying at anchor in the Sound, while Brodir who only had command of twenty vessels anchored just outside. The two Chiefs had a dispute about the ownership of a flock of sheep, and continued to argue about them while at anchor for two days. On the night of the third day, both groups of "Long Boats" were attacked by thousands of what the translater of the saga called "Ravens" that nested on the Calf.

The Vikings fended off the birds as best they could with their shields and swords. The birds, that could only have come from what we now know must have been the vast Shearwater colony, killed one man on each of the boats. The attack, and the death of their comrades, was to the superstitious Vikings evidence of something supernatural, and a warning about the probable outcome of their quarrel.

Another reference occurs in 1337, when the Isles of Scilly were let by Edward III to a certain Abbot Ranulphus for the sum of 6s 8d, or 300 puffins, which valued them at about ¼d each! Its earliest English recording on the Calf was by William Camden in 1586.

The Manx Shearwater is rather smaller than a gull, and, like so many other sea birds, it is dark grey above and white below. It gets its name from its flight just above the water, with stiff wings, appearing to shear the tops of the waves. While on the wing it is one of the most grace-ful and strongest fliers, but on land it is very ungainly, its pink legs being set rather too far back for walking. Like the fulmars and petrels its hooked beak has projecting nasal slots, and like these birds to which it is related, it is known as a "Tube nose".

Two hundred years ago the colony on the Calf was probably the largest in the world and, although up to 10,000 young were at one time being slaughtered for food each year, this had little effect, if any, upon the vast numbers. The harvest took place, according to George Waldron, at the end of July. Bishop Wilson, however, wrote that "about August 15th was the right date", and Thomas Pennant gave the date as being "at the beginning of August". The harvest of "Puffins" as they were erroneously called, was like any other, subject to tithe by the Church. There is a certain rock in the Sound where the birds were counted; it is called in Manx Creg-y-Jaghee.

Some of the accounts of the Earls of Derby show that the Shearwater was of the greatest commercial value. There are several references to feather gathering around the period 1600; a Katherine Moore was paid 26s 8d for twenty stone of them. This additional harvest probably took place after that of the Shearwaters themselves.

There is recorded in the Castle Rushen papers another valuable by-product of the Shearwater, for, in 1599, there is a reference to puffin oil for treating wool, and in 1602 2s 4d was paid for "Puffin Oyle for Armer". Other people also profited from the trade, for in 1600 Richard Browne received 5s for shipping Puffins to England. In 1604 in a list of "Carriages and Ffraights" there is an entry, "Pd. to Ffisher boat for carrieing the puffins to Douglas 11s 6d". The Cooper was also employed, for in 1630 Derby ordered "Puffins in Ffirkins pickled, and Ffirkins scured", to be sent to Knowsley. Puffins were packed in brine like herrings, and were considered to be a great delicacy. It is interesting to recall that the flesh was so fishy in taste that they were a permitted food during Lent in those days.

Shearwaters had another strange use, for they were used as ground rent. Prior to 1644 the Calf of Man, together with Balladoole and Scarlet, belonged to the Stevenson family. In that year the Earl of Derby took over the Calf. He was concerned about the safety of the Isle of Man, so he fortified the Calf and sent over a garrison. He must have felt that some compensation had to be given, for he granted to Richard Stevenson "certain closes, and 500 puffins" yearly. After the execution of the Earl this agreement was confirmed by Charlotte de la Tremouille in 1656. "At the request of Richard Stevenson of ye Isle of Man I do certify that I did seal and execute a deed bearing the date of the 15th day of Sept. 1651, according to a power I then had, and I do further certify that upon the bargain made between my Lord and him, concerning the Calf of Man, there were yearly allowed 500 puffins to him". This agreement was also confirmed by both General Fairfax and his Governor on 20th June and 16th August, 1656. The Stevensons continued to receive this strange ground rent for a further forty years, when the then Governor

Sankey refused to honour the agreement further. For the next five years the family endeavoured to have the rent restored, but in 1704 the matter was finally closed.

Many important people were interested in this valuable bird. James Chaloner, who was one of the Commissioners under Lord Fairfax in 1652, wrote in "A Short Treatise of the Isle of Man" dated 1656, "There is in the Calf of Man a sort of sea fowl called Puffins, of a very unctious constitution, which breed in ye coney holes (ye conies leave their holes for a time) and are never seen with their young but either very early in the morning or late in the evening, nourishing (as it is conceived) their young with oil, which drawn from their own constitution, is dropped into their mouths, for yt being opened there is found in their crops no other sustenance but a single sorrel leaf, which the old give their young for digestion sake (as is congectured). The flesh of these birds is not pleasant fresh because of their rank and fishlike taste, but pickled or salted they may be ranked with Anchovies, Caviar, or the like. But profitable they are in their feathers and oyle, of which they make great use about their wool."

Bishop Wilson wrote, "They will at the expense of wine, spice, and other ingredients to pickle them, make them very grateful to many palates; and send them abroad, but the greatest part are consum'd at home, coming at a very proper time when the Husbandman, who is now throng in his harvest."

The name Manx Shearwater was given to *Puffinus Puffinus* by Francis Willoughby in 1676, in order to distinguish it from the true Puffin or Sea Parrot, *Fratercula arctica grabae*. He wrote in 1678, "The old ones early in the morning at break of day, leave their nests and young and the island itself, and spend the whole day in fishing on the sea, never returning, or once setting foot on the island before evening twilight, so that all day the island is so quiet, and still from all noise as if there were not a bird about." He also wrote, "They feed their young wonderous fat. When they come to their full growth, they who are entrusted by the Lord of the island, draw them out of their coney holes; and that they may more readily know, and keep an account of the number they take, they cut off one foot and reserve it, which gave occasion to the fable that the Puffins are single footed." "They usually sell them for 9d per doz a very cheap rate."

The numbers of young Shearwaters taken was enormous; in 1709, thirteen men spent nine and a half days at the task of "hunting the puffins". Their combined wage was £2-1-6. Two years later, the harvest was "822 dozen and 2", i.e. 9,866. As there was only one young bird to each nest, one can readily estimate the tremendous size of the colony. It must have been a most unpleasant task, as the birds were withdrawn from the burrows with an iron hook.

In 1775 the Shearwaters were still being harvested, for in *A Description of the Manx Parishes,* presumed to have been written by John Quayle, we read, "Within this parish is the Calf of Man, about a mile square remarkable for the birds called puffins, which are birds of passage. In the month of March they come upon the Island and prepare a nest in the rabbit holes and are no more seen till May, when they return and lay one egg only, on which they hatch for six weeks, and in the beginning of August, their youngsters are hooked out of the holes in great numbers, and at the end of the month, are no more seen till March following. The old are about the size and pretty much the colour alike the grey plover, but the young are bulkier, and in perfection while in down, being the greater part fat, which some call delicious, others think Fishy and Raucous, but are generally allowed to be superior to the Soland Goose, and liked by the people.'' John Quayle must also have used Shearwaters as part of his rent, for he wrote to the Duke of Athol in 1774 apologising, ''I have hitherto been prevented from sending my annual tribute of Puffins, I have now forwarded 2 kegs to Grosvenor Place.''

The Manx Shearwaters are true sea birds; they rarely visit the land except at nesting time, when they nest down rabbit holes. While breeding, they are completely nocturnal in their habits, only visiting their nests in the dark. Even the light of the moon is too much for them. However, their instinct and sense of direction is so strong that they can unerringly fly straight to their one nest among thousands even on the darkest night. During the breeding season one of the partners is quite prepared to fly enormous distances in search of food. Birds ringed on the 15,000 pair colony at Skokholm, Pembrokeshire, have been recovered in the nesting season as far away as the Bay of Biscay.

Manx Shearwaters have a homing instinct worthy of the finest racing pigeon. Many experiments have been carried out, but the record must surely be held by the bird taken from its burrow on Skokholm and released in Boston, Massachusetts. This Shearwater returned home in twelve and a half days, having averaged 250 miles a day. This is all the more remarkable because it is far beyond the Shearwaters' normal range.

The birds' nocturnal habits protect them from most predators, although it is estimated that Gulls on Skokholm kill about 2,000 a year.

The exact date of the destruction of the huge Manx colony is uncertain, the probable reason being the confusion of its old name with that of the true Puffin, or Sea Parrot, *Fratercula arctica*. This bird, still present on the Calf, is a small Auk with an orange triangular-shaped beak, quite unlike the Shearwater in appearance, but with similar breeding habits. A number of these were no doubt included in the Shearwater harvest.

There are two theories about the loss of the Colony. Some authorities feel that it was the gradual ousting of the birds from their burrows by the true Puffin. However, it is known, that these two species live and breed quite amicably in other areas. Another argument against this theory is that the colony was completely wiped out in the space of a very few years. The other theory is that the Shearwaters were destroyed by rats eating the eggs and young, as they were down vulnerable burrows, and not on inaccessible cliff ledges, as is the case with so many other sea birds. It is reputed that the rats came from a Russian ship. Richard

Townley in *A Journal kept in the Isle of Man* written in 1791, mentions the wreck of this 700-ton ship in 1786. It is significant that only five years after the date of this wreck, Townley, on a visit to the Calf, purchased from an old man his complete day's harvest of "eight sea parrots", a very small number and by their description obviously not Shearwaters.

In 1811 George Woods, in *An Account of the Past and Present State of the Isle of Man,* was writing about the colony in the past tense. Thomas Quayle, writing in 1812, mentioned the shipwreck as being the reason for the loss, and went on to write, "Not an individual is now bred in the island". Fortunately, there is now strong evidence that, after an absence of about 180 years, this interesting bird has returned to what we would like to consider its homeland. During their period on the Calf in 1959 Einar and Dido Brun, the ornithologists, reported that they frequently saw small numbers of Shearwaters in flight above the sea, and naturally thought that they had come from Skokholm or elsewhere, but one night in June they heard the cry that Shearwaters make to warn their sitting mates when approaching their nests. This experience was reported on several other occasions. The decided to inspect probable sites on the north and west sides of the island, but could find no evidence of nesting. One night, however, above Kione-ny-Halby on the south-east side, they illuminated about fifty birds flying low overhead with their powerful torches. This site was of course a very favourable one for Shearwaters because of the many disused rabbit burrows which were shielded from the beams of the Chickens Rock lighthouse.

On August 16th they reported having seen two on the ground. On the 17th they waited on the cliff and heard the Shearwaters calling continually. This time they were extremely lucky, for they managed to catch one that was foolish enough to land nearby, the first to be caught in its nameplace for over 170 years. It was photographed, measured, and ringed, and eventually released at Gibbdale Bay. On the night of the 19th they caught two more, and heard the sound of a third in a rabbit burrow. This place was carefully marked, and excavated next day, but they did not find a nest. Unfortunately the Bruns were due to leave for home, so they found it impossible to excavate more than a few burrows on the site. In 1968 a few more specimens were caught by members of the Manx Bird Club, but they also failed to find any eggs or young.

Conditions on the Calf now seem to be suitable for the return of the Shearwaters. The myxamatosis outbreak of 1959 and several minor epidemics since have almost completed the extermination of the rabbits, leaving the burrows empty. Another fortunate thing is that the Gulls, deprived of their diet of rabbits, are taking rats. This, together with the efforts of the Observatory staff, has led to a great decline in the numbers of these rodents. Although breeding cannot be proved without the evidence of eggs or chicks, and at the time of writing these have yet to be found, it is most probable that a few pairs have nested. How wonderful it would be if a colony of these, the only birds with a Manx name, could be re-established in their old home on the Calf of Man.

Top: The Manx Shearwater.
*Photo. courtesy of G. Bond. Copyright reserved.*

Bottom: A bird trap in the glen.

**STAMPS** by C.W. HILL

SHAGS AT THE CALF OF MAN

11P ISLE OF MAN

Sea birds and coastal views in the Isle o
Man provide the designs of a new series o
low-value definitive stamps being issued by
the Manx Post Office for ordinary use. The
series comprises 12 values ranging from 1p
to 18p. The 11p stamp (above) shows
shags on the coast of the Calf of Man, the
small island which lies off the south-west
tip of Man. The designs are the work of a
Douglas artist, John H. Nicholson, RI, who
has designed many other stamps, as well
as coins and banknotes, for the Isle of Man.
This is the third definitive series to be
issued since 1973, when the Manx Post
Office became an independent authority
and introduced its own stamps. The other
two series showed general views.

## CHAPTER 8

### FLORA AND FAUNA

... spect the flora of the Calf is similar to that of the
...t there are differences. There is, for instance, a
...es. Apart from an Ash near the Mill, the few trees
...near the farmhouse. In that area there are a few
...a Spruce, Sycamores, and Willows. In the garden
there is a pink flowered Horse Chestnut. Near both Jane's House and the
farmhouse the common Fuchsia which grows so well on the Isle of Man
is to be found. An attempt has been made to plant a few trees nearby and
protect them from rabbits with netting. Some of these have died, and the
remainder are doing very poorly.

It is interesting to see at Jane's House an Elderberry, or Trammon
as the Manx call it. The leaves of these trees were considered in olden
times to be a specific against evil influences. At funerals they were
thrown onto the graves, and sometimes carved upon the headstones. On
the main island it is rare to find a *Tholtan,* or ruined cottage, without
a Trammon nearby.

The botanist is fortunate in being able to find in the small area of
the Calf a variety of terrain which adds greatly to the interest. There are
cliffs and rocky places near the sea, areas of poor thin soil underlaid
by rocks or glacial drift, marshland, an old mill dam, a pond, disused
arable land, and once-cultivated gardens, hillsides of heather and
bracken, stone walls, and both sheltered and very exposed areas. Each of
these yields a variety of plants adapted by nature to the prevailing conditions. As far as may be ascertained no detailed study of the plant life
has ever been made. It would be most interesting if this could be done,
and a real comparison made with the flora of the Isle of Man nearby.
The list of flora at the end of this chapter is far from complete. There
are many plants on the Calf other than those mentioned.

Perhaps it should be mentioned that in the now completely
neglected front garden of the farmhouse, which is now the Observatory,
there is still growing a *Rosa centifolia.* This delightfully scented rose
which was once common on the porches of Manx cottages is now some-

thing of a rarity. Still surviving are some cultivated Foxgloves and a clump of Oxalis, called in the Isle of Man "Sunshine Sally", while on the roadside nearby there is a large patch of the Rose of Sharon.

A description of the fauna on the Calf is a light task, as they are few in number. The Brown Rat is thought to have been brought to the Calf when a Russian ship was wrecked in the Sound in 1786. At one time the Calf was infested with these rodents, but their numbers have now diminished.

The Rabbits, a proportion being black, used to be seen in large numbers and formed one of the principal items of revenue at the time of the Athols. Myxomátosis, probably introduced by a diseased carcass being dropped by a bird, decimated them for a time as it did on the Isle of Man. They now seem to be on the increase once more.

The Pygmy Shrew and the Woodmouse are to be found, and the Observatory staff have had to remove long-eared Bats from the nets at times. These may have come from the Isle of Man as there is no evidence of them residing on the Calf.

There are also stories of wild (domesticated) cats, and wild goats, but there is no evidence of these either. If they do indeed exist, they are relics of the days when the Calf was farmed. In his day, the owner, Mr. Haigh, frequently brought new cats over to control the rats, but they quickly died off. He agreed that there were feral goats on the island when his father took over the farm, but as they damaged the crops they were hunted and shot. Mr. Maddrell once caught a mouse that lived in the kitchen; it was the only one. He also caught a weasel in a rat trap which again was the only example. These were probably imported from the main island, possibly in animal feeding stuffs, seed corn, or seed potatoes.

The grey Seal is quite a common sight. A favourite place for seeing them is while the are swimming in the area just east of the separation between the Burroo and the Calf. They do come ashore on to the rocks of the island, and are thought to breed.

In other chapters there are several references to sheep on the Calf. In the old days these would have probably been the native Manx Loaghtan breed. There seem to be several ways of spelling this word. It can also be seen spelled Loghtan, Laughtan, and also Laughtyn.

It is thought that these sheep were brought to the Isle of Man by the Vikings. They are like the Soay breed in appearance. Similar sheep to the Loaghtan being found in both Iceland and St. Kilda would lend credence to the theory of Viking importation.

The Loaghtan sheep are small with rather long legs. They get their name from their brownish fleece, loghtan meaning a dark colour. It is said that the fleece contains rather more hair than wool and it is this same white, undyeable hair that is seen in genuine Harris tweed.

The rams are splendid animals with four or sometimes even six horns! A writer in the sixteenth century said, "The Manks sheep have tails of almost incredible magnitude". Joseph Train wrote in 1845, "These hardy little creatures are of mean appearance, with a high back, narrow ribs, and tails somewhat resembling that of a goat. In the whole breed, a general distinctive mark is said to appear, in a brownish coloured patch on the back of the neck. In traversing the island in the summer of 1836, I could only observe in the uplands a few of these starved looking animals. . . . When shorn, eight fleeces, unwashed, average seven pounds of wool.''

In Chapter 9 reference is made to the wildness of this breed, and the difficulty that the Duke of Athol had with them. This characteristic wildness of the Loaghtan is mentioned in the history of the Manx Church. It was extremely difficult to fold them in order to take the tithe. ''Anyone that hath sheep or lambs that cannot be brought to fold for the purpose of taking the tithe, then the Proctor hath used to depose them upon a book, what wool and lambs they hath, and so to pay truly the tithe thereof.''

In an endeavour to ensure the survival of this unique breed of Manx sheep, a small flock, the property of The Manx Museum and National Trust, was first of all subjected to an inspection by a veterinary surgeon to make sure that the sheep were in perfect health. In 1969 they were taken over and released on the Calf. This small flock consisted of four ewes and one ram. In the spring of 1970 each of the ewes had a lamb, so that the flock now numbered nine. One of the ewes unfortunately died, so that with another four lambs born in 1971 the number in the flock rose to twelve, seven ewes and five rams. In the spring of 1972, no less than seven lambs were born. The flock has been left to roam the Calf at will, in a completely natural way, with one exception. In order to strenghthen the breed, the original ram was returned to the main island in 1972 and a fresh one brought over.

The object of setting up a small flock on the Calf, apart from the interest and knowledge to be gained from their progress, was to protect them from any possibility of extinction by disease. Apart from those that are the property of the Manx Museum and National Trust now on the Calf, there are several small flocks on the main island. The National Agricultural Centre at Stoneleigh Abbey, Warwickshire, also has a flock of twelve ewes and two rams. The Rare Breeds Survival Trust has offered financial help to a new society for Loaghtan sheep called in Manx *Sheshaght ny Kiree Loaghtan*. It is to be hoped that the sheep in Warwickshire, together with the forty-five on the Isle of Man and the fifteen at present on the Calf, will not only survive but increase and become as well known as the Manx cat!

Some Flora found on the Calf:

| | |
|---|---|
| *Acer* | Sycamore |
| *Achillea millefolium* | Yarrow |
| *Achillea ptmarmica* | Sneezewort |
| *Ajuga reptans* | Bugle |
| *Alchemilla arvensis* | Field Lady's Mantle |
| *Anagallis arvensis* | Scarlet Pimpernel |
| *Arctium intermedium* | Lesser Burdock |

| | |
|---|---|
| *Armeria maritima* | Sea Pink |
| *Asplenium marinum* | Sea spleenwort |
| *Athyrium filix-faemina* | Lady Fern |
| *Bellis perennis* | Daisy |
| *Brassica nigra* | Mustard (black) |
| *Calluna vulgaris* | Heather Ling |
| *Capsella bursa-pastoris* | Shepherd's Purse |
| *Cardemine pratensis* | Cuckoo-flower |
| *Cenastium viscosum* | Mouse-ear Chickweed |
| *Chenapodium album* | White Goosefoot |
| *Chrysanthemum leucanthemum* | Bull Daisy |
| *Chrysanthemum segetum* | Corn Marigold |
| *Cochlearia* | Scurvey Grass |
| *Cotyledon umbilicu-veneris* | Wall Pennywort |
| *Digitalis purpurea* | Foxglove |
| *Drosera rotundifolia* | Sundew |
| *Echium* | Bugloss |
| *Erica cinerea* | Bell Heather |
| *Erodium maritimum* | Sea Stork's Bill |
| *Erythraea centaurium* | Centaury |
| *Euphrasia occidentalis* | Eyebright |
| *Fraxinus excelsior* | Ash |
| *Galium verum* | Yellow Bedstraw |
| *Glaux maritima* | Sea Milkwort |
| *Hedera helix* | Ivy |
| *Heracleum sphondylium* | Cow Parsnip |
| *Holcus lanatus* | Meadowsoft Grass |
| *Hydrocotyl vulgaris* | Marsh Pennywort |
| *Hypericum pulchrum* | Slender St. John's Wort |
| *Hypericum tetrapterum* | Square-stalked St. John's Wort |
| *Hypochoeris radicata* | Cat's Ear |
| *Jasione montana* | Sheep's Bit |
| *Juncus effusus* | Soft Rush |
| *Juncus sylvaticus* | Jointed Rush |
| *Lasterea filix-mas* | Male Fern |
| *Lastrea aristata* | Broad Buckler Fern |
| *Lemna minor* | Duckweed |
| *Leontodon autumnale* | Autumnal Hawkbit |
| *Leontodon taraxicoides* | Lesser Hawkbit |
| *Lonicera periclymenum* | Honeysuckle |
| *Lotus uliginosus* | Great Birdsfoot Trefoil |
| *Lychnis dioica* | Red Campion |
| *Lychnis flos-cuculi* | Ragged Robin |
| *Lythrum* | Purple Loosestrife |
| *Matricaria inodora* | Scentless Mayweed |
| *Mentha aquatica* | Water Mint |
| *Myosotis palustris* | Forget-me-not |
| *Narthecium ossifragum* | Bog Asphodel |

| | |
|---|---|
| *Nasturtiun officinale* | Watercress |
| *Oenanthe crocata* | Water Dropwort |
| *Onicus arvensis* | Creeping Thistle |
| *Onicus lanceolatus* | Spear Thistle |
| *Onicus palustris* | Marsh Thistle |
| *Pedicularis sylvatica* | Red Rattle |
| *Peplis portula* | Water Purslane |
| *Phyllititis scolopendrium* | Hart's Tongue Fern |
| *Plantago lanceolata* | Ribwort Plantain |
| *Polygala vulgaris* | Milkwort |
| *Polygonum heterophyllum* | Knotgrass |
| *Polypodium vulgare* | Polypody |
| *Potomogeton polygonifolius* | Bog Pondweed |
| *Potomogeton natans* | Pondweed |
| *Potentilla anserina* | Silverweed |
| *Primula vulgaris* | Primrose |
| *Prunella vulgaris* | Self-heal |
| *Ranunculus acris* | Meadow Buttercup |
| *Ranunculus ficaria* | Lesser Celandine |
| *Ranunculus repens* | Creeping Buttercup |
| *Rubus fructicosus* | Blackberry |
| *Rumex acetosa* | Sorrel |
| *Rumex obtusifolius* | Common Dock |
| *Sagina procumbens* | Procumbent Pearlwort |
| *Salix aurita* | Willow |
| *Salix cinerea* | Sallow |
| *Sambucus* | Elder |
| *Somolus valerandi* | Brookweed |
| *Scabiosa succisa* | Devil's Bit Scabious |
| *Scilla verna* | Vernal Squill |
| *Sedum anglicum* | English Stonecrop |
| *Senecio jacobaea* | Ragwort |
| *Senecio vulgaris* | Groundsel |
| *Silene maritima* | Sea Campion |
| *Spergula vulgaris* | Corn Spurrey |
| *Spergularia rubra* | Red Sand Spurrey |
| *Spiraeq ulmaria* | Meadowsweet |
| *Stellaria media* | Chickweed |
| *Taraxacum vulgare* | Dandelion |
| *Teucrium scorodonia* | Woodsage |
| *Thymus serpyllum* | Wild Thyme |
| *Trifolium repens* | Clover (White) |
| *Ulex europeaus* | Gorse |
| *Urtica dioica* | Nettle |
| *Viola riviniana* | Dog Violet |
| *Veronica officinalis* | Common Speedwell |

Top: Grant's Harbour. Cow Harbour is just beyond the storehouse.

Bottom: South Harbour with lighthouse store.

# CHAPTER 9

## HISTORY AND
## AGRICULTURE

The first real ruler of the Calf was, of course, the same as that of the Isle of Man. His rule can be said to have begun with the Second Scandinavian period, when in 1079 Godred Croven I established his dynasty. The Calf continued to have the same owner as the main island until Sir John Stanley II succeeded to the Lordship of Mann in 1414.

Very shortly after that, the Calf of Man came into the possession of a Manx family that can trace their connection with the Isle of Man back to the year 1302. They are the Stevensons (in some old documents spelled Stephenson) of Balladoole, or Balladowle as it was then called. The exact date of the change of ownership is not known. Sir Ralph Stevenson, G.C.M.G., the present senior member of the family, stated that several generations of the Stevensons owned the Calf before their name appeared in the Manorial Roll of 1511. He also said that evidence of this early ownership was to be found in some fragments of old Manorial Rolls that were found in Castle Rushen in about 1930, and now in the possession of the Manx Museum. Unfortunately the exact date of these is not known, so the Sheading Roll of 1417/18 had to be examined to find the evidence needed. ". . . 31st May 1418 . . . Reginald Stevenson complains against John McFale, on a plea of unjustly taking and keeping one cow value 40d, who comes and places himself on the inquisition by whom he was found guilty. Therefore in mercy 12s, and ordered to pay the price." "John McFale complains against the said Reginald, on a plea that he unjustly kept Vld of the tithe of the said Reginald belonging to the Church of St. Columba, and the aforesaid Reginald came and said that the case should be heard in a Church Court, and seeks judgement on this, and the case is sent to the Bishop by the Judges' decision, and the said John is in mercy for his wrongful plea."

There is another interesting item about the Calf in the Sheading Roll. On the 4th October 1417. "Inquisition taken on a trespass made in the Calf on the oaths of Morris McAceyn, Thomas McGillon, William Nicolson, Robert Tailour, Adam McNicoll and William McKeown, who says that Thomas de Yvenowe and Gibbon McWady have four pigs on the Calf contrary to regulations, and that Michael Shirlok has two there, and say that John Shirlok has cut brushwood there. And therefore they are in mercy.''

The name Reginald Stevenson also appears in the Indenture of 1417/18 between ''The Commissioners of Lord de Stanley Lord of Mann and the Deemsters and Keys of Mann''.

The earliest dated record of the ownership of the Stevenson family that appears in the *Liber Assedationis,* or Manorial Roll, is dated 1511 and refers to the Lord's Rent paid to ''Thomas Earl of Derbie, Lord Stanley of Mann''. It reads, ''Le Calf. From Thomas Stevenson for 1 Island called The Calf demised to him as above 26s 8d.''

The Calf remained in the ownership of the Stevenson family until 1644. It was then bought by James the 7th or ''Great'' Earl of Derby, who wished to fortify it against the Parliamentarians. The Great Earl had every reason to fear for his possessions, for, being a Royalist, they were at great risk. He had raised a small fleet of Manx vessels, and in one encounter drove off three Parliamentary ships which were trying to land troops on the Calf. In another naval battle he was able to defeat no less than five Cromwellian men-of-war. After the 7th Earl was executed at Bolton, the Calf with the Isle of Man came under the jurisdiction of the Commonwealth, and it remained so until the Restoration, when, in 1660, it was restored to Charles Stanley, the 8th Earl of Derby.

In 1666 the Earl once again tried to establish deer on the Calf, other attempts having failed for various reasons. From his herd on the main island, he sent over two males and ten females. It would seem that the attempt was once again unsuccessful, for no more is heard of deer for thirty years. One might be led to think that perhaps he was experimenting with the wrong breed—Fallow deer perhaps? Red deer are so hardy that the Calf of Man would seem a very mild environment for that type.

However, the Earl was responsible for the introduction of the rabbits which were to play such an important part in the economy of the island. The first account that can be found of rabbits being hunted is in 1670. Ferrets were used for the purpose. It is rather surprising to read that the ferrets were fed on corn and meal of various kinds. They are usually considered to be decidedly carnivorous!

In 1672 the Calf became the property of William, the 9th Earl of Derby. The Earl seems to have made a determined effort to deter the poachers, for in the Exchequer Book under the date 1687 there appears, ''Certaine orders sett down by Robt. Heywood Esq. Gov'r of the Isle of Man . . . that no maner of person or persons whatever, shall presume to go unto the Calf Isle by day or night, under any pretence whatsoever, to annoy destroy and carry away the Lord's game there, under the penalty of forfeiting the sume of iiiL (£3) sterling to the use of the Right Honble Lord of this Isle, and to endure such corporal punishment as the nature of the offence will deserve''.

Although deer did not seem to thrive on the Calf for one reason or another, sheep certainly did, for in 1694 the flock on the island consisted of no less than 86 lambs and 310 adult sheep, together with 15 assorted goats. One would imagine that the Calf would prove to be ideal for the latter. Another attempt seems to have been made to estabiish deer, for in 1696 there were 36 adults and, no doubt to the Earl's satisfaction, 6 fawns.

In 1702 the Calf passed to James, the 10th Earl of Derby. During his ownership the Calf continued to provide a good return, for in 1705 no less than 80 lambs were gelded. There is no mention of the total size of the flock. The rabbits also seem to have become well established, as one might expect! In fact 256 were caught.

Some crops seem to have been grown, for in 1707 someone was paid for making kelp rakes. The kelp, or wrack as it is called in the Isle of Man, was used for fertilizer. In 1712, although there is no reference to lambs, forty-eight muttons were shipped to the main island. Rabbits seem to have been a regular source of revenue, for George Waldron in his book *A Description of the Isle of Man* wrote, "Rabbits are in such plenty, especially in the months of August and September, that they may be bought for 1d a piece, returning the skins which are the perquisite of the Earl of Derby, and given to his steward who sends them to England and Ireland by persons who come over every year on purpose to import them. The tenant on the farm on the Calf annually advertises the shooting, which induces many strangers to visit for that purpose."

One of the hazards of living the sporting life on the Calf was described by Maxwell Frazer in his book *In Praise of Manxland.*

> "For rabbits hot and rabbits cold
> For rabbits young and rabbits old
> For rabbits tender rabbits tough
> I thank the Lord I've had enough!"

James, the 10th Earl of Derby, unfortunately died without issue, so in 1736 the Isle of Man and the Calf came into the possession of James, the 2nd Duke of Athol. This Duke was the grandson of Amilia, Countess of Athol, who was herself the daughter of James, the 7th Earl of Derby.

The returns from the Calf did little to enrich the Duke. "An account of the several particulars of the produce, or income of the Calf Isle for the years following *viz:*—

**DEDUCTIONS**

| 1741 | For herbage | 5- 9- 0 | Thos. Woodworth and partners for hunting the puffins | 1-12- 8 |
|------|-------------|---------|------------------------------------------------------|---------|
|      | rabbetts | 2-15-10 | | |
|      | muttons | 3-10- 3 | Thos. Woodworth for meat & corn for the ferrets and a man assisting him hunting the rabbetts | 14- 8 |
|      | rabbett skins | 4-15- 0 | | |
|      | puffins | 5-10- 4 | | |
|      | | £22- 0- 5 | | £2- 7- 4 |

| 1742 | For wool | 1- 7- 0 |
|---|---|---|
| | herbage | 3- 0- 6 |
| | rabbetts | 2- 4- 4 |
| | muttons | 4-19- 6 |
| | rabbett skins | 4-17- 6 |
| | puffins | 4- 8- 4 |
| | | £20-17- 2 |

| | |
|---|---|
| Thos. Woodworth hunting the puffins | 1-12- 8 |
| Thos. Woodworth meat & corn for ferrets, man assisting him hunting the rabbetts | 15- 8 |
| Wattleworth Lambfell 3 ferrets | 19-10 |
| Thos. Colley bringing 2 boat loads lime 2 boat loads timber to Calf for repairs | 1- 0- 0 |
| Thos. Clague, Thos. Holmes for taking down the roof of Woodworths house & making a new one | 3-10- 0 |
| Jo. Keone for slating sd. house | 1-12- 5 |
| Jo. Keone for plastering | 10- 0 |
| Wm. Quayle Thos. Radcliffe and partners for repairing the keepers house | 12- 6 |
| 3 doz nails for flooring the house | 2- 0- 0 |
| Sundry persons clipping sheep | 4- 7 |
| | £13-13- 8 |

| 1743 | For wool | 3-19- 2 |
|---|---|---|
| | herbage | 3- 3- 6 |
| | rabbetts | 2- 0-10 |
| | muttons | 3- 3- 0 |
| | rabbett skins | 3-17- 6 |
| | puffins | 5- 4- 1 |
| | | £21- 8- 9 |

| | |
|---|---|
| Thos. Woodworth hunting puffins | 1-10- 0 |
| Thos. Woodworth clipping sheep | 4-5½ |
| 15 stoars for the puffin hunters | 1- 0 |
| Thos. Woodworth meat & corn for ferrets and a man helping him | 12- 0 |
| Keepers yearly salary | 3-10- 0 |
| Ferrymans yearly salary | 2- 0- 0 |
| | £7-17-5½ |

| | |
|---|---:|
| 1741 Neate produce for this year | 14- 2- 9 |
| 1742 Neate produce for this year | 1-13- 6 |
| 1743 Neate produce for this year | 13-11- 3½ |
| Medium as it now stands | 13-17- 0 |
| from which to be deducted | |
| incidents & repairs | |
| reconid to be | 1- 0- 0 |
| | |
| Neate rent as it now stands | £12-17- 0 |

Apart from the strange spelling and even more strange arithmetic that the Duke seems to have passed without comment, some interesting facts emerge from these accounts. One is that we tend to forget that inflation is no new phenomenon. A year's salary for the Keeper in the middle of the 18th century was about equal to a week's salary in 1939. Another interesting thing is that the "rabbett" skins were worth more than the rabbits, and the 3 dozen nails at £2-0-0 were vastly more expensive than they are today; the reason being that they had to be made by hand, one at a time, by the local blacksmith. One cannot imagine that the Duke would have been very pleased with the "neate medium" rent of £12-17-0 for the whole of the project on the Calf, which was less than four times his keepers' wages.

Governor Lindsay seems to have been rightly concerned about the very poor income that the Duke received, for he wrote about a scheme for obtaining a better return by replacing the Manx Loaghtan sheep with a different breed. "The sheep that are now upon it are so very wild there is no catching of them to clip them, without hunting them with doggs and in taking them several of them jump into the sea and are lost. It is impossible to make anything of sheep, unless they are constantly herded. It is therefore submitted to your Grace, whether these sheep, which are reduced to be as near be guessed to between eighty and ninety, for they are so wild that they cannot count them exactly, should be sold, and a new stock of breeding sheep from Galloway of their small kind purchased." He went on to say that he had had an offer from a shepherd to work the new sheep for twelve shillings a year. It was estimated that the Calf could support 400 ewes, and an appropriate number of tups. The return would be:—

| | | |
|---|---:|---:|
| 200 lambs at 2/- | | £20-0-0 |
| After 2 years 100 muttons at 4/- | | 20-0-0 |
| Wool | | 10-0-0 |
| | | £50-0-0 |
| From which should be deducted | | |
| Interest on the stock & carriage | | |
| to the Calf £160 | 8-0-0 | |
| Salary | 1-0-0 | |
| | 9-0-0 | 9-0-0 |
| | | £41-0-0 |

This scheme was not proceeded with, for another opportunity to increase the revenue presented itself. On February 19th, 1745, a Lawyer, John Humphrey of King's Bench Walk, London, wrote to the Duke and enquired from him his terms for a tenancy of the Calf. A week later the Duke wrote to Governor Lindsay enclosing Humphrey's letter. He asked for advice as Humphrey was a total stranger to him. Humphrey, it would seem, proposed to build a house on the Calf, and practise law on the Isle of Man. Lindsay's advice was that if Humphrey would stock the Calf with sheep himself, a fair rent would be £25-0-0 exclusive of the rabbits and puffins, the right to prospect for minerals and erect miners' houses to be reserved to the landlord. The Duke seems to have been suitably impressed with the prospect, for on April 2nd, 1745, he sent Governor Lindsay a copy of a lease of the Calf for 21 years that he had signed. He seems to have struck a shrewd bargain, for not only was the rent set at £30, but the cost of the ferryman and keeper would be saved as their services were to be discontinued. Mr. Humphrey, the new tenant, seems to have been well thought of at that time, for a Thomas Brandish wrote to the Duke on September 6th, 1746, that Humphrey had come to England from Ireland, where he had been an Attorney at the Court of Exchequer. "He will bring a good sum for investment on the Calf".

The Duke seems to have been unfortunate in his choice of tenant in spite of his cautious enquiries. Five months later, having sold all his wild Loaghtan sheep, he was chagrined to find that Humphrey had not put in an appearance, nor had he placed the flock of sheep on the Calf that the Duke relied upon for security for his rent. Lindsay wondered if the Duke should repossess the Calf. It was later found that, in spite of the fact that no rent had been paid, Humphrey had appointed a Douglas merchant to be his local agent. After being pressed to pay, Humphrey wrote to say that he had temporary financial difficulties. The Governor was of the opinion that the Duke should cancel the lease. Another tenant had been found, a Mr. D. Forbes of Douglas. Mr. Forbes promised to stock the Calf with sheep to act as security; he would also like to enter into a financial agreement to divide the island into three parts by means of dry stone walling. Governor Lindsay seems to have had the Duke's interest at heart, for he did not let the matter of Humphrey lie. He demanded payment of the outstanding rent from Humphrey's local agent, who then claimed that the first £30 had been paid by note of hand! The Governor was not satisfied. He advised the Duke that this stratagem to delay matters might lose him the prospect of an excellent tenant in Forbes, and went on to say that he had heard that Humphrey's agent had been selling the rabbit skins from the Calf. As usual the law seems to have taken a very slow course, for another four years were to elapse before we find that Humphrey was now too poor to pay the outstanding rent, and offered some property in Fleet Street, London, as security for a mortgage. After a further three years Humphrey, who was still being pressed, offered £40 in final settlement. This was no less than nine years after he had first made his unfortunate attempt to take over the Calf.

On December 9th 1751, a Mr. Cochrane offered to take up the lease at £30 a year. Nothing further is heard of Forbes; it would seem that the splendid opportunity to let to him was lost.

In those days it was thought that rapacious landowners waxed fat on the returns from their estates. At least as far as the Calf was concerned, this was far from being the case. During the period 1741 to 1751, the Duke's total revenue had only been £78-11-0, or an average of £7-17-1, a paltry sum even in those days.

In 1754 another attempt was made to settle deer on the Calf. For the first time it is confirmed that they were Fallow Deer. There is no evidence about how they fared.

Ten years later, in 1764, the Calf came into the joint ownership of the 3rd Duke of Athol and Charlotte his wife. In 1773 the Duke and Duchess granted a lease of the Calf to John Quayle of the Creggans, for a period of 21 years at an annual rental of £30. They reserved to themselves, however, all the mineral rights. John Quayle was to play a very important part in the development of the Calf. He was much respected on the main island. For his time he was a very well read and learned man. He was interested in archaeology, which was a fortunate thing, for in the first year of his tenancy the Crucifixion Stone was found.

It was in Quayle's time that the first real attempt was made to use the Calf as an agricultural holding. John Quayle seems to have been on excellent terms with the Duke, for he wrote to him on December 19th, 1773, saying that he was sending the Duke a stallion and two mares and that he was also sending two small kegs of puffins as a gift. He reported that he had twenty-one men employed on the Calf, building a wall right across the island. He had ten fallow deer at the Creggans awaiting shipment to the Calf. He proposed to establish red grouse on the island, but up to now had been unable to obtain any. He was, however, confident that the Calf would be an ideal environment for them.

It is rather interesting to hear about the many attempts over the years to establish deer, for these always seem to have failed. However, there is a clue in several references to poachers in the old records. No doubt they were at least partly responsible. There are also records of deer swimming the Sound at slack water and raiding the crops on the main island. The chance of their being allowed to return must have been rather remote!

During John Quayle's tenancy of the Calf he is supposed to have built a banquetting hall for the entertainment of his friends. If he did indeed build one, there is no trace of the building to be seen now.

David Robertson in his book *A Tour through the Isle of Man,* written in 1794, describes the Calf at this period of its history, and how he sailed from Derbyhaven to South Harbour. During his visit he saw many gulls, wild pigeons, and puffins. The island was stocked with black cattle. A shepherd that he met told him that at one time there had been a large stock of sheep, but the number had been greatly reduced by the nightly depredations of poachers from the main island. The herds of Red and Fallow deer had all disappeared. While walking round the island,

Robertson saw many hare, partridge, and heath game, which he under-stood gave amusement to the sportsmen who visited the island for the shooting. The rabbits that he observed in great abundance were of con-siderable value for their skins, which, together with the feathers of the sea birds, were worth more than £200 a year to the owner, the Duke of Athol. The return from the Calf would seem to have greatly increased from the £30 which Quayle's lease, just ended, had brought in. One cannot help thinking that Robertson must have been misinformed. He went on to write that during his ramble he found no human habitation, except the shepherd's hut which was much decayed. He cannot have been very observant, or his ramble very extensive, for only five years earlier Peter Fanning's map showed two houses diagramatically in the area of South Harbour but probably meant to represent the main house and 'Jane's' house.

John Feltham in his book *A Tour through the Isle of Mann in 1797-1798* describes how he visited the Calf in 1797. "The excursion to the Calf is generally made from Port Iron, from which it is about three miles (vide Kirkchrist Rushen Parish). Its surface is rather barren, so that I cannot descant on its picturesque scenery; everything bearing the character of the sublime, tending rather to raise the bolder emotions of the mind, rather than amuse it with gentle sensations. The eye is regaled from its heights, with the azure vault of heaven, and beneath, the briny surface is covered with swelling sails, either impelled with the cheerful breeze, or agitated by bleak winds, or scowling storms, while the sur-rounding surface of the ground presents a verdure wild and innocent."

> "Just where the distant coasts extended curve,
> A lengthen'd train of sea fowl urge their flight.
> Observe their files, in what exact array
> The dark battalion floats, distinctly seen
> Before yon silver cliff, now, now they reach
> That lonely beacon, now are loft again
> In yon dark cloud. How pleasing is their flight."

"Round the Calf you see innumerable quantities of sea birds, wild pidgeons etc. The quantity of herrings etc. they annually destroy, are supposed to be some hundred thousand barrels."

The rent of the island continued to increase, for the next record, dated 1799, is a lease to John Summers, who had offered £60 a year for it, together with a piece of ground at the smelting mill (probably at Derby Haven). The tenant was to pay all repairs. Poachers on the Calf still seem to have been a problem, for the lease required the landlord to "defend him from persons going upon the Calf shooting the rabbits". The actual rent of the Calf alone was £45 less £1-15-0 for conveying the sheep there.

The next tenant was a Mr. Gourley. George Woods in his book *An Account of the Past and Present State of the Isle of Man,* written in 1811, mentions him in the chapter that he devotes to the Calf. He said that Port Erin was the best place to hire boats at that time, either small sailing boats or ones with four rowers. The cost was from seven to ten shillings according to the length of stay on the Calf. As he passed Kitterland he saw a flock of sheep on it. Mr. Gourley, the tenant, explained to Mr. Woods that his new house was not quite finished; it was to be very commodious. His present house was to be ultimately turned over to his farm labourer. Mr. Gourley, his wife, and the labourer, were the only inhabitants. The island belonged to the Duke of Athol, and he was glad to report that he was not subject to tithe. There was a field of grass, two of oats, and a plot of potatoes. There were eight or ten cattle, a similar number of horses, and a few score sheep. With the exception of those in the farmer's garden, there was not a tree or shrub on the island more than three feet high, and those in the garden only reached six feet.

The rabbits were the chief source of profit; he caught 2,000 a year. For this purpose he used about 100 common rat traps. Others were caught in a 200 yard vertical net, which was stretched across between the pasture and the area of the rabbits' burrows. In the season Gourley also harvested the sea birds' eggs, sometimes taking as many as 300 in an hour. Woodcock were taken too. He had also imported hares in the hope that they would breed, "but he never saw one of them again". At the time that Woods visited the Calf, Mr. Gourley had engaged extra staff for the harvest. "The day that I spent on this retired but hospitable island was the harvest home or 'meller' (mhelliah) of the Manks, a time of Jubilee. The labourers had plenty of ale, and the master dealt out his excellent rum with a cautious, not sparing hand. Though of ten or twelve people all were merry, none was absolutely intoxicated. A dance in the barn concluded the festivity of the day."

All this was just about seven years before the first pair of lighthouses were brought into service in 1818. A year later in 1819 an advertisement appeared in the Gazette, "To be sold ship's blocks, spars, small sails etc. Apply Mr. Lorrimer, Calf of Man, or Charles Scott, North Quay, Douglas." As Mr. Gourley was still the tenant on the Calf, one would assume that Mr. Lorrimer must have been one of the first lighthouse keepers.

John Gourley, who had been so generous with his hospitality at the time of the harvest home described by George Woods, unfortunately fell on hard times, for on July 27th, 1820, he was reduced to advertising in the Manx Advertiser, the sale of his stock, crop, and furniture. He wrote to the Duke of Athol a few weeks later and asked to be relieved of his tenancy, which had proved to be a burden for "it was more than seven years before the Calf produced as much food as maintained my family one year . . . I have lost over the rocks and otherwise between five and six hundred pounds' worth of horses and cattle, but particularly sheep, not less than fifty some years died of the rott. I have put in more than 10,000 yards of drainage. I have laid out more than £3000 on the Calf, and now all is sold but the crop which is the best I ever saw on the Calf. I have raised from 16 to 18 tuns of good hay this year."

The Duke seems to have been very lenient with poor Mr. Gourley, who had done so much to improve the farm, for James McCrone, writing from Castle Mona only two weeks later, was able to inform him that he had re-let the Calf to a Mr. Dawson who offered £106 a year for a fourteen year lease. The lighthouse keeper was also interested in renting the island, but his offer was only £100 a year so it was rejected.

A great change was now to take place in the ownership of the Calf, for in 1828, following the Revesting Act of 1765, the sale of the Calf to the Crown was completed. *A Valuation of and a Report on the Isle of Man* was published. An abridged version of the part relating to 'The Calf Island' follows:—

## THE CALF ISLAND

Mathew Dawson tenant, let on lease for 14 years from 12-11-1820, consists of a good dwelling and farm buildings in tolerably good condition. The rent £106. Arable land 40 acres. Rabbett warrens 548 acres. Total 588 acres. Annual value £92-10-0.

£92-10-0 at 25 years purchase amounts to £2312-10-0.

*Observations*   Divided by Kitterland. Difficult access.

1400 rabbetts at 1/- a pair, also carries 300 sheep, great losses during winter.

\*     \*     \*     \*

## THE LIGHTHOUSES

The Commissioners of Northern Lights tenants. Let to them for ever at a rent of £40. There are two lighthouses, and about 12 acres of land for cows, which hardly find sufficient pasturage during the summer months.

12 acres.                    Annual value £40.

£40 at 25 years purchase amounts to £1,000.

*Observations*   Remarks about the fine quality and maintenance of the towers and buildings. The rent is liberal and more than the land is worth.

The Arbitrators for the sale of the Duke's rights to the Crown raised the following query. "If the total annual rent was £146, why had the valuers submitted a value of £185?" McCrone, the Duke's agent, replied that the reason for this was that the Calf was "extra parochial" and therefore not subject to tithe. Also it was now possible to improve the land by the application of lime from the quarries at Port le Mari. In 1828, after a period of ninety-two years in the hands of the Dukes of Athol, the Calf of Man passed into the possession of the English Crown. It would seem that the Crown was really interested in the sovereignty of the Calf rather than the actual ownership, for on September 6th, 1831, only three years later, it was advertised for sale. "Calf Island Crown property, at present let to Mathew Dawson at the yearly rent of £106. Lease expires 1834. Abundance of lime to be had at Port-le-Marie so that the land can be improved at very little expense" (abridged) "The annual value of the rabbits is said to equal the rent". On January 24th, 1832, the commissioners for Woods, Forests and Lands sold the Calf to William Leece Drinkwater, whose descendants still live at Kirby, Braddan.

The prospect of traffic to the Calf seems to have increased at about this time, for the following advertisement was inserted in the *Manx Sun* on May 14th, 1833.

## ALBION HARBOUR SOUND OF THE CALF

The public are respectfully informed that two ferry boats (to prevent their being disappointed) are placed at the harbour which is the shortest distance between this island and the Calf, and they will be in readiness at all times to convey passengers, cattle, and luggage, to the Calf . . . etc. etc. From the shortness of the distance, from five to ten minutes will be the usual time for crossing. The boats are constructed to land the passengers with great ease. The proprietor pledges himself that the boatmen shall be sober, and steady men, and any of them behaving with incivility will be immediately discharged. A ferry house will soon be built, and all necessary refreshments provided at moderate terms. Carriages can at present proceed to Cregneish, and from thence to the harbour is only a short distance, with a pleasant prospect and a footpath.

This ferry will be found by visitors wishing to go to the Calf of Man a great convenience, as they will always be able to get there, when it would be impossible to go from Port St. Mary and Port Erin. A road is commenced from Cregneish, and carriages will soon be enabled to go the whole way to the harbour. The boats will be furnished with fishing tackle, bait etc.. and every care will be taken by the proprietor to study the favours of the public.''

This rather optimistic advertisement is of interest, for it places on record the commencement of the tourist traffic that now brings thousands of holiday-makers to see the magnificent view of the Calf across the Sound, and the large number that each season visit the Calf from Port Erin and Port St. Mary. It also gives the date of the construction of the Cregneish/Sound road.

It was in 1834 that the storehouse and road from South Harbour to the lighthouses was built, for an advertisement appeared in a Manx paper, "Contractors are invited to tender for a road and storehouse on the Calf. The site will be pointed out by Mr. Dawson, principal lighthouse keeper." It is safe to assume that this was the Mathew Dawson who was also tenant of the Calf, unless there were two persons of the same name. As already noted, there are several references to the light-keepers being interested in the tenancy. Mathew Dawson seems to have had his tenancy extended for two years, for as mentioned previously, it was granted in 1820 for fourteen years, which only brings us up to 1834.

The *Manx Sun* of August 12th 1836 carries an advertisement, "To be let the Calf Island, apply Mrs. Drinkwater". The ownership of the Calf had again changed, for in 1836 William Leece Drinkwater died and in his will left the Calf to his wife, Charlotte, and his heir, his daughter, Eleanor. On August 26th, 1836, the same newspaper is used again. "To be sold on the Calf of Man the stock and effects etc. of Mr. Dawson, the tenant on the Island". The next reference is also to be found in the *Manx Sun*. It is dated February 3rd, 1837, and names the new tenant as a Mr. Shepherd, who "requests tenders for the quarrying and landing on the Calf of Man 300 tons of limestone". In the *Advertiser* there appears an interesting announcement, "Married, Mathew Dawson late of the Calf Island, to Martha a daughter of the late William Clarke of the Cumberland Tavern".

The elaborate arrangements made for a ferry in 1833 seem to have failed, for Mr. Shepherd, the tenant, set up his own ferry in 1839, and announced in the *Advertiser* that "Boats and Boatmen are always available". In 1839 Mrs. Drinkwater, who was, of course, a wealthy woman, would seem to have become short of ready money for some reason, for on January 1st Charlotte and her heir, Eleanor, granted the Calf as security for a mortgage of £1050 to James Holmes. The Calf was still the property of Mrs. Drinkwater in 1845, for Joseph Train states that in his book of that date. Eleanor Drinkwater, who inherited the Calf, married a Lt. Colonel Clarence Horatio Carey of Castletown.

By 1851 the Calf seems to have become quite a thriving community, for the census of that date shows a population of thirty, including the lighthouse keepers, farm labourers, and their families.

The ownership of the Calf was now passed down in the Carey family for about sixty years. In 1867 Woods' Atlas shows the Calf, less the portion that was in the possession of the lighthouse authorities, as belonging to Charles Horatio Carey. In 1878 the owner was Col. George Carey, who, among other things, had been a London barrister. It was he who wrote, "I would rather live on the Calf in my lifetime, than go to Heaven when I die". George Carey built the present farmhouse and most of the adjacent buildings. The house is a well built stone structure. Above the porch is a Latin inscription, *PARVA DOMUS MAGNA QUIES* "Small House Great Peace". Col. Carey lived in some style, keeping several servants and a gamekeeper, whose wives and families formed quite a population. He paid no taxes until he was foolish enough to apply to the Manx Court to protect him against trespassers. The proceedings brought to light his favourable position, so he was promptly taxed! Like all the other owners and tenants, he trapped and sold the rabbits. He also installed an alehouse for his retainers! George Carey was a great athlete and a famous oarsman. He is reputed to have been able to row across the Sound when the eight-knot current was flowing. He actually died while returning from a visit to Castletown. Mrs. Carey, who must have had a rather lonely life, did embroidery as a hobby. This was in silk and wool, backed by Manx handwoven linen/wool cloth. Examples of her work are still in existence.

About the year 1900, Carey let the farming of the Calf to a Thomas Clague, who was a well-known businessman from Port St. Mary. Clague built and ran the Belle View Hotel, Port Erin, and later the Perwick Bay Hotel, Port St. Mary. As he also owned a butcher's business, he was interested in sheep, so he wisely appointed an Isle of Skye shepherd called McLeod to manage the Calf Farm for him. Clague wasn't a man to neglect any opportunity to turn an honest penny, so he used the vacant lighthouse buildings for accommodation for Catholic priests to spend a few days on the Calf during their stay at Belle View. Tommy Clague, as he was called, farmed the Calf until 1909.

By 1905 the Calf had passed into the possession of W. L. Carey, who lived at Derby House, Castletown. He had inherited from his brother. On June 11th he wrote to his Solicitors on the subject of a possible sale of rights on the Calf to the Marconi Company. In this letter he stated that his brother, who had lived on the Calf for thirteen years, had been "Lord of the island and practically its Monarch, he would allow no one to land without permission. There are no taxes. If a vessel is wrecked on the Calf and the crew leave it, the vessel becomes the property of the owner of the Calf". The Marconi Company cannot have been impressed with the opportunity to use the Calf as a wireless station, or with its other advantages, for we hear no more of them.

W. L. Carey must have been the William Leece Drinkwater Carey whose marriage had ended in divorce and who, only five years later in 1910, while living in San José, California, sold the Calf to Samuel Haigh for £2,650. In 1909, a year before he sold at the end of Clague's lease, Carey appointed a steward, Edward Moore Maddrell, to run the farm, harvest the valuable rabbit crop, and look after the Calf generally. Maddrell took up residence at the farm with his young wife, formerly Mary Ann McLeod, who was to prove to be ideally suited to the rather isolated life, probably because she was the daughter of the shepherd from the Isle of Skye who had farmed for Clague. With them they brought their one year old son Jack. To Jack Maddrell we are indebted for an account of his twenty-three years' association with the Calf, from which it is possible to form a very good idea of what life was like on the island at that time.

The Maddrells had only been on the Calf for about a year when W. L. Carey sold to Samuel Haigh. Sam Haigh, as he was called, was a wealthy business man in the clothing trade. His home was in Quarmby, near Huddersfield, Yorkshire. He had four daughters and a son, and like many other Lancashire and Yorkshire people at that time, had formed a great affection for the Isle of Man. Guided by Edward Maddrell's experience, Haigh decided to run the Calf as a general farm, but to specialise in beef and mutton, as milk production was contra-indicated because of transport difficulties. The Maddrells only kept about two cows in milk to provide milk, butter and cream for their own use. A pair of horses was kept for ploughing the then twenty-eight acres of arable land, and for general cartage. On the fenced-in sixty-one acres of pasture land, they kept a bull, a few store cattle, and about a hundred sheep. The arable land was used to produce oats and other crops for animal feed stuffs. Two pigs were kept for their own use. The bacon and ham were properly prepared with salt and saltpetre, and not just pickled in brine as was the custom on some Manx farms at that time. A Mr. Gorry used to come over specially to kill the pigs and dress them. They had the usual farm implements, horse-drawn plough, disc-and-chain harrows, hayrakes, etc. They also had hay and turnip cutters, and 'stiff' carts as they are called in the Isle of Man. In those early days there were no tractors, but they did have one later, and towards the end of their stay even a Trojan van.

An attempt was made to make electricity by driving a dynamo by means of a wind vane set up on the hill behind the farm near Bushell's House. The first vane was rather like an aeroplane propellor, but when this failed they tried the type sometimes used to pump water. The wind however was much too strong, and as there was no governor the dynamo frequently burned out! The whole contraption was then moved down the hill nearer to the farmhouse, but the same trouble was experienced; either the vanes were broken, or the dynamo was destroyed. A last effort was made by reducing the height of the tower by half, but on this failing, the scheme was abandoned and the farm was once again reduced to paraffin lamps! The remains of the tower can still be seen.

The Maddrells had excellent transport facilities to the main island. Two rowing boats and a small motor boat were kept at Cow Harbour. Later, when the lighthouse tender was replaced, Haigh bought the old one. This was based at Port St. Mary and used for heavy work. Five tons of coal in 1 cwt. bags were brought over at a time, landed at South Harbour, and taken up to the farm by cart. Seed potatoes and oats were also brought over, together with the paraffin, building materials, and other heavy goods. The sheep were also transported by the South Harbour to Port St. Mary route. As mentioned earlier, the cattle had to swim across the Sound at slack water from Cow Harbour to the main island.

The Farm had two sources of water. A spring at the back led into an underground cistern, and this fed two taps, one in the back kitchen and the other in the farmyard. This was used to water the animals, especially the horses that drank water in large quantities. There was also an iron pump just across the road in front of the house. This was ultimately replaced by a semi-rotary pump. This water was pumped up into a tank in the attic, and used for a bath and W.C. upstairs. Water was rarely short, but if in a dry summer it tended to fail, the washing was taken down to the lower lighthouse which had a tank fed by rainwater.

Before the indoor toilet was installed, the labourers used to use a two-seater earth closet behind the left (lower) part of the house, and the family used a single one behind the main house. One doesn't need to tell a Manx reader that this important place is called a *Thie Veg* or Little House.

Light goods and provisions were brought weekly from Port Erin. In the summer, if the sea was calm, they used to row from Cow Harbour to Port Erin, but in winter they just rowed across the Sound. When conditions permitted, which wasn't very often, Mrs. Maddrell then had to walk up the steep road towards Cregneish, over the Mull Hill, past the stone circle, and down an even steeper hill into Port Erin, a distance of over three miles, carrying a heavy basket of surplus butter and eggs. After these had been sold, she bought provisions such as sugar, tea, and dried fruit, and then carried them back another three miles to the Sound. Even then she had the best part of a mile to walk home from Cow Harbour. Edward Maddrell once walked over this route carrying twenty-six rabbits and three hares slung around his shoulders.

Of course in the winter, and even in summer, there were many occasions when the Maddrells were stormbound. They always had plenty of food in stock for such an emergency. As Mrs. Maddrell, like most Manx farmwives, used to bake her own bread, they always used to keep

1 cwt. of flour in hand. They were, apart from such items as tea and sugar, almost self-supporting. They had bacon and ham, always the two best rabbits, chickens and ducks: home-baked loaves, soda bread and cake, milk, cream, butter, and eggs. Mrs. Maddrell unfortunately never had enough spare milk to make cheese. Feeding the dogs was no problem as they were fed on the small or poor rabbits. Mr. Haigh built a greenhouse in the back garden to grow tomatoes and they also grew the usual kitchen-garden vegetables. There was even a small rose garden at the back.

All the cooking was done on a coal-fired kitchen range and a Valor paraffin stove. At times Mrs. Maddrell had to cater for large numbers, the Haigh family as well as her own, building workers and extra help at harvest time. But Jack could not remember any help in the house. They had other men to help on the farm from time to time. Jack Maddrell could recall a Ned Christian who used to be there almost permanently between the years 1914 to 1919. Harry Kelly, whose name is so well known because of the preservation of his cottage at Cregneish, used to come onto the Calf at certain times of the year to help to catch the rabbits.

Shortly after arriving on the Calf the Maddrells had another child, G. McLeod Maddrell, who lived there until he died at the age of about twenty-two.

As in the days of the Athols rabbits were an important source of revenue. The Maddrells caught them by a rather simple method. The fields of pasture were surrounded by excellent stone walls. There were about ten holes left in these. At the appropriate time of the year, the holes were left open for a few days and then closed at dawn. Two fox-terriers were then released in the field to be worked. The dogs promptly chased some of the rabbits and killed them. This caused the others to cower down in fright and 'freeze'. The other dogs and the men themselves used to round up the remainder. The dogs became so exhausted with the killing that they had to be rested from time to time. The largest catch was 240 in a day. The rabbits were shipped to Liverpool, but during the first World War they were used to feed the German internees at Cunningham's Camp.

One of the worst problems on the Calf was the rat population. People at Cregneish used to call it 'Rat Island'. The rats that had come ashore so long ago from the Russian ship that was wrecked in 1786 had thrived and these were joined by others that are known to have come from the wreck of the *Clan McMaster*. Crude poisons like Rodine were used—Warfarin had not been developed then. Dogs and traps disposed of a few. Mr. Haigh tried several times to increase the number of cats by bringing in new ones, but for some reason these normally hardy creatures failed to thrive. They died of a form of distemper or cat 'flu. Another bright idea was to buy a mongoose, but the authorities on the main island heard about this and persuaded Mr. Haigh to abandon his plan. The Maddrell boys used to hunt the rats for sport, using the two terriers.

They sometimes managed to catch twenty to thirty. The terriers would even chase and kill the rats in the sea!

Mr. Haigh built the silo near the farmhouse. At that time there was only one other on the main island. This belonged to Mr. Cunningham at Ellerslie, Marown. The mill was in a ruinous condition, but Mr. Haigh had the mill dam made wider and higher than it had been. This gave a greater expanse of water. Wild duck used to land there and provide good shooting. There were also snipe to be shot in the vicinity.

It was interesting to learn that the smithy had been built by the original lighthouse keepers. The buildings alongside used to house their cows. The fields adjacent to the lighthouse were also part of that property. It was rather poor land in Maddrell's day.

It was Mr. Haigh who converted the lower lighthouse into a dwelling. It was for the use of his daughters. The six building workers lived up at the farmhouse. He must have been disappointed to find that the girls used to prefer to live with the Maddrells, no doubt attracted by Mrs. Maddrell's good Manx cooking!

Jane's House was barely habitable. It was repaired and occupied for a time by labourers building a dock near Cow Harbour. Mr. and Mrs. Haigh used to go to Jane's House for picnics: they claimed that the water from the seepage spring made the best tea that they had ever tasted. An old earthenware crock of the type used at that time to keep bread or herrings in was sunk into the ground up to its rim to collect the water.

On being asked if he had ever seen any sign of the *keill*, Jack Maddrell said that, apart from the oval of stones at South Harbour, he had never seen anything. He did say, however, that he had never deliberately looked for one. The grave near Bushell's House, he said, was that of the son of one of the lighthouse keepers. The child had died of scarlet fever. Some people are of the opinion that the keeper thought that part of Bushell's House might have been a *keill,* or that he had heard of this theory, and buried his child in the vicinity. The poor man may have thought that it was the nearest thing to consecrated ground that he could find.

During the 1914/18 War, there was a signal station on the flat area above the Sound on the main island. Jack frequently used to communicate by semaphore, but never had to do so in an emergency. The lobster boats from Port Erin always kept a lookout towards the Calf, but there was no definite system in use for attracting attention. However, they did have another contact, for Tommy Woodworth would call once a week from Port Erin with the mail if the weather permitted.

Jack Maddrell stated that the farmhouse was very sheltered from all directions but one, and that the Calf generally was one or two degrees warmer than the main island. Two interesting experiences on the Calf were recalled. The first one was during the 1914/18 War. Mr. Haigh had permission to burn the rough grass off the Big Piark provided that the fire was extinguished before dark. Unfortunately, just at dusk the wind got up and the almost dead fire burst into flame again and got completely out of hand. The fire was seen by the Manx Coastguards, who informed the police. A party of police obtained a boat and landed on the Calf. They made their way in the dark up to the farm to help to extinguish the fire. The reason for the concern was not aircraft in those days, but German U boats. When the fire was eventually put out it was so dark that the police could not find their way back to their boat and the two boys had to guide them back. Mr. Haigh was prosecuted and fined £20, quite a large fine in those days.

The second experience was the wreck of the *Clan McMaster* in 1923 which has been described in another chapter. The ram which the Lascar seamen took with them on to the Calf escaped and made its way up to the farm. The Maddrells chased it in order to keep it away from their stock. Just then the Lascars appeared in hot pursuit, and promptly thought that the Maddrells were trying to steal it! As neither could speak a word of the other's language, the parties became quite heated, and trouble was only prevented by the appearance of a ship's officer.

Jack Maddrell did not live on the Calf the whole twenty-three years. He lived there from the age of one until he was eight. His parents taught him his early lessons. At the age of eight the Education Authority insisted on proper schooling, so he went to Demesne Road School in Douglas, living with his aunt. He later stayed with another aunt and went to Rushen school. He proved to be a good scholar and finished up at the Castletown Grammar School, living at the home of the headmaster. He was then apprenticed as an engineer at Gellings Foundry, South Quay, Douglas. Of course he always returned to the Calf for the school holidays to help his father on the farm.

It was during the ownership of Sam Haigh that the first reference to the buildings on the Calf being liable for rates appears. These rates were very low and the total was only £15-6-1½.

On July 13th, 1931, a year before the Maddrells left, Haigh sold the Calf of Man to Joshua Appleyard Popplewell and his wife Ethel, for the sum of £3,000. The advertisement for its sale is of interest to historians, because it gives a very good description of the farm and the other buildings and facilities on the island at that date. For this reason it is included in full.

| | |
|---|---|
| *House* | 2 sitting rooms, dairy, pantry, four bedrooms, and boxroom. |
| *Farmhouse* | Kitchen, back kitchen, 3 bedrooms. |
| *Buildings* | Stable, hay loft, barn, pigstyes, 3 cowhouses, 2 outhouses, cart shed, coach house, poultry house. New Silo, paddock, and kitchen garden. |
| *Lower lighthouse* | Converted into dwelling, dining room, kitchen, scullery, pantry, bathroom, 3 bedrooms, boxroom, Smoking room in lighthouse, and gardens. |
| *Jane's Cottage* | Three rooms on ground floor. |
| *South Harbour* | Wharf and storehouse. |

71

| | |
|---|---|
| *Approach from Calf Sound* | Newly constructed wharf which can be approached at high or low tide, also boathouse that can be approached with slide and winch. |
| *Roads* | A road that runs straight across the island to the lighthouses, and also down to South Harbour. |
| *Water Supply* | Is ample. |

The advertisement also mentioned that there were 89 acres of fenced-in land, 61 of these being pasture and 28 arable.

Popplewell bought the Calf because he thought that the fresh air would be beneficial to his son who was suffering from Tuberculosis, a disease from which he eventually died. The Maddrell's only stayed with Popplewell for about a year. They left the Calf in 1932 after twenty-three years in charge of the farm. Popplewell then appointed Frederick Corkish to be his steward.

Joshua Popplewell was a wealthy man and was quite prepared to spend money on improving the island that had become his home. He made many improvements to the farm buildings and other facilities. However, the principal drawback to living on the Calf was found to be the lack of means of communication with the main island, especially with an invalid son to look after. He therefore decided to instal a telephone. Little did he know the problems that he would have to overcome. The engineers decided that first of all a normal line would have to be carried on poles from Cregneish to the Sound. A heavy underwater cable would then have to be laid across the water with its mill-race tides, and a further normal line on poles would connect Cow Harbour with the house. The telephone line from Cregneish presented no difficulty—it was just normal telephone work. The underwater cable, however, was most expensive to provide and lay, and many technical problems had to be solved. Once contact was made with Cow Harbour, Popplewell and the technicians thought that the rest would be just routine, but they were to find otherwise. From Cow Harbour to the house is roughly a mile, and over sixty poles were needed. The difficulty that the Post Office engineers had to overcome became apparent when they started to erect the first pole, for under a bare covering of gravelly soil was solid rock! Practically every pole had to be set in a hole that had been blasted out. One cannot help thinking that if Popplewell had only started at the Calf end instead of at Cregneish, the project would not have progressed beyond the first few poles! Even when completed at great expense, the service was a failure. The engineers had under-estimated the rip of the notorious current. So after the main cable had been fractured and repaired several times, the ambitious scheme had to be finally abandoned.

Popplewell lived on the Calf for about five years. Then one of those strange coincidences occured that so often change the course of history. Popplewell boarded a Manchester train and found himself sitting in the same carriage as an acquaintance of his, Francis Joseph Dickens. Dickens, who, incidentally, was a distant relative of the famous author, more to make conversation than out of real interest, asked Popplewell how he was getting on on the Calf. To his horror he was told that

Popplewell had almost completed a deal to sell the Calf to a syndicate who proposed to form a company to exploit the island as a tourist attraction. Dickens, who was a great lover of the Isle of Man and especially the peace and natural beauty of the Calf, was absolutely appalled at the very idea, and said to Popplewell that he would offer £500 more than the syndicate had done on condition that Popplewell gave him a firm decision before they left the train. Fortunately Popplewell agreed.

F. J. Dickens made sure that the Calf of Man would be protected from development and vandalism for all time, for he generously gave the Calf to the National Trust for Places of Historical Interest or Natural Beauty. What we now call The Manx Museum and National Trust did not exist in 1937. One thing is certain and that is the gratitude of the Manx people. Their appreciation was expressed when the Governor and Tynwald presented Mr. Dickens with an 'Illuminated Address'.

There is a little mystery about the deeds. The sale by Popplewell is dated February 27th, 1937, and conveys the Calf to a Donald McLeod Matheson for the sum of £3,000. In a deed dated July 20th, 1937, Matheson presented it to the National Trust. There is a confirmatory deed, signed by Popplewell and his wife, dated August 1st, 1937. There is no mention of Dickens anywhere. The explanation of this would seem to be that at first Dickens wished the gift to be anonymous. In other words Dickens provided the money and Matheson, who was the secretary to the National Trust, was only a nominee. However, a secret like that could not be kept for long, and the name of the real donor soon became known. F. J. Dickens' daughters have erected a bronze plaque at Cow Harbour, stating how the Calf of Man has been preserved for all time. The Manx people owe a great debt to this generous man. The Calf of Man with its wild beauty of heathland and rugged cliffs, its flowers and birds, and above all its peace, is preserved for their enjoyment for ever.

The date when Mr. Corkish, who was appointed farm steward by Mr. Popplewell, gave up the post, is unknown. It was probably in 1936. In 1937 the steward was Robert Garrett. There are no records of his farming activities, but he does deserve a mention for posterity, for in that year his fourth child was born on the Calf, the first for over fifty years. His fifth child was also born on the Calf, although this was not intended. In 1939 the Garretts found that there was to be another addition to the family, and Mrs. Garrett was determined that this time her child would be born in the Maternity Hospital on the main island. However, this was not to be. Firstly they had to contend with bad weather which prevented them crossing the Sound, something that they had hoped to do in plenty of time. Then Mr. Garrett had an accident. Another attempt had been made to create electricity by means of a windmill and generator. Mr. Garrett mounted the small tower to lubricate the shaft, but carelessly forgot to immobilise the mill. A sudden gust of wind caught the propeller, and one of the blades caught him in the groin. This was so painful that it was impossible for him to row the boat to take his wife over. Once again he had to act as doctor and midwife—he must by now have been quite experienced! On March 21st, 1939, a son weighing seven and a quarter pounds was born.

Mr. Garrett must have had his hands full with a farm, a wife, four children, and a baby to look after. It was most fortunate that around this time two of their friends arrived. They were a Mr. and Mrs. Pixton of Kirk Michael, who kept a dinghy on their side of the Sound. Mrs. Pixton quickly took charge and sent her husband back to Port St. Mary to obtain various necessities and a supply of provisions, which were running low. Mrs. Pixton stayed on the Calf with the Garretts for a few days to give all the help she could.

This experience and the problem of their ever-growing family made the Garretts decide to give up the job as Warden and steward of the farm. They did, however, offer to stay on until replacements could be appointed by the National Trust. The Trust advertised the post as "the loneliest job in Britain", and to their surprise and astonishment received no less than 900 replies. The political situation in 1939 with the prospect of another World War may have had something to do with it. A rather pathetic article was written at this time for the *Zionist Weekly,* by an author who could not help comparing conditions in the British Isles with those prevailing at that time in Germany, where the Jews were suffering all kinds of persecution and humiliation. He described as "a breath of fresh air" the news of this advertisement. "The job of the man appointed will be to protect the wild birds on the island, and this will be a lonely life, yet there were over 900 applicants, and I could not help saying to myself, great are the people who, in the midst of a world of woe can turn their minds to the thought of safeguarding the welfare and comfort of the birds on a secluded island off their shores."

Once the Trust had got over the shock of the number of applicants they whittled them down to a short list of three, and wisely decided to send them and their wives over to the Calf to study for themselves the conditions under which they would be expected to live. They thought that the reactions of the wives would probably be the determining factor in making their choice. Mr. D. M. Matheson, the Secretary to the National Trust, said, "We came to the conclusion that it would not be fair to send anyone out, without making doubly sure that they knew what they were in for. The job is looking after 615 acres of bird sanctuary and running a farm. It will probably be one of the loneliest in Britain. It is not the husband we worry about as much as the wife. None of the candidates as far as we know has lived alone on an island before. We think we have the right three in the final selection. A National Trust official has been put at the disposal of the candidates who have been chosen to see the island. He will guide them round and see their reactions."

Robert Mitchell was the first candidate chosen to inspect the island and its facilities, and he made a thorough examination in the company of Mr. Gibbs, the Assistant Secretary, H. M. Rodgers, a member of the Manx Committee, and K. Williamson, a noted ornithologist. The party stayed on the Calf for four hours, and among other things inspected the stock of 200 sheep, several cattle, and two horses, still being looked after by Mr. Garrett. It was explained to Mitchell that should he accept the post it would be no easy task; looking after the animals alone would be really a full time job. In addition to her other work, Mrs. Mitchell would be expected to supply light refreshments to the holiday-makers that could be expected on day trips during the summer season. Little did they know that six years were to elapse during the 1939-45 war when summer visitors would be conspicuous by their absence. It was also pointed out to Mitchell that he and his wife might be marooned for weeks on end by the high seas, and that there were no proper means of communication. The telephone installed by Popplewell at the then tremendous cost of £2,000 had finally broken down, and would be too costly to repair. There is no trace of the visits of inspection of the other two candidates on the short list. Perhaps they had second thoughts about the job.

Robert Barton Mitchell was duly appointed Warden of the Calf in May, 1939. He was an Irishman, but came to the island from Spilsby, Lincolnshire. He was the son of a clergyman. In a letter that he sent to a Lincolnshire paper, he wrote that his job would be to preserve the island in its natural state, as a beauty spot and a natural breeding ground for birds. He would also have to protect the plants and the birds' nests from egg stealers, keep in touch with ornithologists, and safeguard the interests of the National Trust. The island would be closed to visitors during the nesting season, with the exception of ornithologists with special permission. Later on during the holiday season they expected holiday visitors on day trips from Port St. Mary and Port Erin. The Calf was well worth a visit as it was a place of great beauty in a lovely setting. It was covered with heather, much of it white. Mr. Mitchell seems to have been concerned about his ability to keep the egg poachers at bay, for in the same letter he asked if anyone could supply him with an Irish Wolfhound puppy!

In August, 1939, a few months after Mitchell arrived on the Calf, a postal service of a kind was set up by Mr. Gibson, the Head Postmaster of the Isle of Man. There were to be three deliveries a week, weather permitting. The mail was to be taken over by J. Jackson of Port St. Mary. Jackson claimed to have had six years' experience with the Sound, having frequently taken supplies over. He claimed that the stories about the Calf being cut off by bad weather were greatly exaggerated and that he expected no difficulty. He must have been chagrined when he was "forced to eat his words", for Mitchell was frequently cut off, on one occasion for no less than six weeks! As mentioned earlier even on the calmest day there always seems to be a swell in the Sound. When it was calm enough to cross, but the swell too high to permit a landing, Jackson used to put the letters in a bucket, and while a helper fended him off the rocks with a boat hook, he would pass the bucket to Mitchell slung on the end of an oar! The hazardous postal service must have been a godsend to Mitchell, as it was his only means of communication.

He started his life on the Calf with his mother. His wife did not join him until September, just on the outbreak of war. He had had a little company in August for the Trust let the old converted lighthouse to a

Mr. and Mrs. J. H. Howarth of Chorley, Lancashire, in order that they might spend a few weeks' holiday there.

When war broke out on September 3rd, 1939, Mitchell realised that he would have to make plans and take precautions against isolation and the shortages of food for his family and the farm animals. He intended to stay on the Calf whatever happened. He therefore made a visit to Port St. Mary with a list of supplies that he would need if he became cut off for any length of time. Among many other goods he ordered 12 tons of cattle cake, and 3 cwt of flour. It took a boat seventeen trips from Port St. Mary to bring it all over. He wisely thought that it might be difficult to obtain the quantities that he needed once rationing had been introduced and he had to be prepared to "stand a siege".

In December, 1939, the Mr. Howarth who had spent a holiday on the Calf during the previous August, decided that the old lighthouse that had been converted into a dwelling by Mr. Haigh would make an ideal refuge for his family if the Germans carried out their threat to bomb the British towns and cities. He brought over his wife and children, a boy of fourteen, a girl of eleven, and a baby. They brought all the family pets with them, a dog, a cat, and, as if there were not enough birds on the Calf already, two tame pigeons. His idea was that the family should live on the Calf permanently, and that he should visit them as often as he could be spared from his business as a cotton merchant. He arranged that their provisions would be brought over by the boat from Port St. Mary that brought those of the Mitchells. Mrs. Howarth decided to devote herself to her children's education, and arranged for correspondence courses to be sent out.

Robert Mitchell and his wife stayed at their post right through the War, in spite of their many difficulties. He could do very little real farming during that period because of shortages of all kinds. During his stay he restored the electric light, which was a great boon. His method was simple and most effective. He drove a dynamo by means of a belt from his tractor, and set up a bank of 12 volt car batteries in an outhouse. Robert Mitchell stayed on the Calf from 1939 to the beginning of 1951, when he left to farm Ballayelse in Ronague on the main island.

In 1951 there occured another important event in the long history of the Calf of Man, for its administration passed into the hands of the Manx Museum and National Trust. It was, however, and at the time of writing still is, the property of the National Trust for Places of Historical Interest and Natural Beauty.

Unfortunately, after the Mitchells left, in spite of extensive advertising, the Calf was left without a warden until April 7th, 1952. Unlike 1939, there were very few applications for the job, and only one of these proved to be suitable. That was the application of Frederick James Faragher. Fred Faragher, as he was called, was a very widely experienced farmer. He had been born in Surby on the main island, and had helped his father to farm Balnahowe until he was twenty-one. He then joined the Liverpool City police force, and was awarded the Police Medal for bravery in 1909. Faragher then went to Australia and for twenty-one years managed a large sheep station there. In 1933 he returned to his native island and farmed at Poyllvaash, retiring in 1947. After his active and varied life his retirement proved to be a burden to him, and although now sixty years of age he re-started farm life on the Calf, fulfilling an ambition that he had had ever since he was a boy. In his own words he "expected it to prolong his life".

Although it was only fifteen months since Mitchell left, he was surprised to find how much the farm had deteriorated. "The place is derelict, it's a shipwreck of a place—everything has gone to seed", he said. The farmhouse and the various buildings had been boarded up. It was estimated at that time that they were worth £20,000, but one would think that that was a gross exaggeration.

Fred Faragher fully intended to cultivate the farm and rear sheep. The first thing he did was to take over a tractor and eighty Scottish ewes and lambs. He did not have a very auspicious start. On his second day he crossed to the Calf with his wife and his son, Norman, with a load of goods, but when the time came to return, in spite of all their efforts, they could not get the engine of the boat to start. They made their way back to the other side of the island and signalled the Chickens Rock lighthouse. The lighthouse keepers then contacted their headquarters at Port St. Mary, who duly turned out the lifeboat at 7.15 p.m. It was 11.55 p.m. before the lifeboat was able to return to Port St. Mary with the Faraghers ignominiously in tow!

Fred Faragher and his wife farmed the Calf until October 1st, 1954, when declining health made Fred give up at last. They were still in residence when the next warden took over.

Lieutenant-Commander Frank Williams was a very different kind of man from the experienced Manx farmer, Fred Faragher. Although not Manx, Williams had been connected with the Isle of Man since he was about ten years old, his parents having brought him over in 1917. He joined the Navy as a boy seaman in 1923, and the fact that he was able to rise by numerous promotions to his present rank in the executive branch of the Navy—no mean feat in his day—is indicative of the tough enterprising kind of man that he is. Williams lived with his wife, Marian, on the Calf during the years 1954 to 1958.

Frank Williams retired from the Navy in 1953 having survived two of the greatest Naval tragedies of the 1939-45 war. He was one of the survivors when the battleship *Royal Oak* was torpedoed in Scapa Flow by the German submarine ace, Prien. He later survived the sinking of the new battle-cruiser *Repulse* by Japanese torpedo-bombers off the coast of Malaya. After retiring, his love of the Navy and its life could not be forgotten, so he became the Commanding Officer of the Manx Sea Cadets.

Frank Williams, unlike one of the previous wardens, Robert Mitchell, who had been chosen from 900 applicants, heard about the vacant job on the Calf by chance during a conversation on Port St. Mary breakwater. Knowing that the Calf of Man was now under the administration of the Manx Museum and National Trust, he phoned Deemster

Kneale who, with the late Deemster Sir Percy Cowley, was able to convince the Trust of his exceptional qualifications for the job.

The post of warden on the Calf, with its freedom and isolation, was to Williams exactly what he had always longed for during the dark and dangerous years of the war. Mrs. Marian Williams was a real country lover; she was thirty-nine at the time and was just as excited as he was at the prospect of living on the Calf. There was only one snag. Like most Naval officers' wives of the period, she had no furniture, having followed her husband around during his career living in furnished flats all the time. She spent an enjoyable and exciting period buying at auction sales all the furniture that they were going to need. Her husband, who had absolutely no knowledge of farming, consulted the late Mr. Howie, at that time the Advisory Officer to the Board of Agriculture and Fisheries at Knockaloe Experimental Farm.

Frank and Marian Williams took over the Calf on October 1st, 1954, and duly took up residence in the rather rambling white farmhouse situated in the hollow in the centre of the island, sheltered from all but the southerly winds. They used the room on the right of the entrance as a lounge, and the one on the left as a living room. The kitchen was in the low part of the building to the left. They used the bedrooms above the main part of the building themselves, and those over the low part for storage. Only one living room had a wooden floor; all the other ground floor rooms had stone floors. They insulated the carpet from the stone with a thick layer of newspapers and a felt. The fireplaces and kitchen range worked very well, and as long as they kept the fires going they were very cosy even in the worst winter weather. They were fortunate in having the inside toilet and bathroom, but in times of water shortage had to resort to the *Thie Veg* at the back!

The transport of their numerous belongings to the Calf was a problem that would have daunted anyone but Frank Williams, who brought to bear all the organising ability acquired during his thirty years in the Navy. It was no ordinary removal from one home to another; everything had to be shipped over by small boats, nct only furniture and personal belongings but farm implements and farm animals, to say nothing of their Labrador and white Bullterrier. The first thing to ship was obviously the tractor and trailer, otherwise how were the goods to be moved from South Harbour to the house? The first snag was quickly encountered, for the President tractor was too large and heavy for the boat! The only thing to do was to dismantle it, bring it over in three pieces, and re-erect it on the other side. Once that had been done and the trailer shipped, the rest of the big job went like clockwork. Two boats were used, one manned by John Gawne, the coxswain of the local lifeboat. The whole operation took three days, the boats making several trips from Port St. Mary each day.

In view of Frank Williams' lack of experience, Mr. Howie advised him to take his time, and not rush into trying to raise crops or keep too many animals. The first farm animals to be brought over were twenty Scottish Blackface ewes and a Border Leicester ram. A sow in pig, a young boar, and sundry poultry were also shipped across. To these were added a cow in milk and another due to calve that were bought from the outgoing farmer, Fred Faragher. Williams had few implements to start with. The tractor and trailer, a rotavator, a potato ridger, a set of harrows, an old 1915 reaper still in excellent condition, and a seed fiddle.

Marian Williams found housekeeping much to her liking. It was really her first proper home. She usually managed to get to Port St. Mary once a week for shopping. Her first task was to lay in an emergency supply of tinned food in case they became cut off. Fortunately this was never required, as the longest time that they were isolated on the Calf was three weeks. Like the other wardens before them they quickly became virtually self supporting. They grew all their own vegetables in the back garden, (Haigh's greenhouse had by now completely disappeared) and collected excellent watercress from the spring in the lighthouse fields. They had their own milk and eggs and quickly learned how to make excellent butter. Mrs. Williams confessed that although she tried hard, her attempts to bake bread were not very successful. She eventually decided to buy a week's supply in Port St. Mary, and freshened the loaves by means of the old trick of soaking in milk and placing in a hot oven for a while. Cooking facilities were very good; there was a three-burner Calor Gas cooker, and also a kitchen range with an open fire. For meat they had their weekly supply from Port St. Mary and also their own poultry, bacon, ham, and pork. Like the Maddrells they had their pigs killed and properly cured for them by someone who came over for that purpose. In an emergency they always had the rabbits to fall back on but they very quickly became tired of these. Frank Williams was a great fisherman and at times absolutely filled the boat with cod. These were split open, salted, and dried in the sun Norwegian fashion. They were then stored in an empty bedroom.

Fuel presented no problem other than that of hard work. They brought their paraffin for the Aladdin lamps over in 5-gallon drums, and their coal in 1 cwt. sacks. Their difficulty was not loading at Port St. Mary as they always had plenty of willing helpers, but in unloading unaided at the Calf. These heavy items, and the animal foodstuffs bought at Castletown, had to be lifted out of the boat onto the wharf, and then lifted into the trailer. At the farm they had to unload, stow away, and then go down to the boat again for another lot.

Frank Williams was an enterprising character. He quickly came to the conclusion that the provision of coal was not only expensive but one of the heaviest jobs that he had to tackle. Why buy it when other sources of fuel were available free? Were the inlets not full of driftwood? Hadn't he heard that peat was once dug? He quickly found peat and cut and dried it in the traditional way. This was used both on the kitchen range and on the open fire in the living room. He was sorry to find, however, that it was not as good as Irish peat. Driftwood on the other hand was a great success. Not only was it most plentiful, ranging in size from fire-wood, to logs and heavy baulks of timber, but, if one was an ex-sailor, easy to obtain. Their method was simple. They would go down to an inlet and collect the wood in a suitable place, laying it within the loop of a steel cable attached to the tractor. When enough had been gathered, the tractor would pull the loop tight and haul the load up. It was then loaded on to the trailer and taken up to the farmyard for storage. During his stay on the Calf, Williams never bought more than a ton of coal a year. This was only used to get a good fire started before laying on the wood and peat.

Their sources of water were still the same as they had been in Maddrell's time. The stone cistern in the back now led into a tank in the attic through a ball valve, and from there to the upstairs bath and toilet. The cistern also supplied the boiler in the kitchen range which gave excellent hot water, and a tap in the yard for watering the animals. Maddrell's semi-rotary pump from the well in the front of the house no longer worked very well. The height of the tank above the well seemed to be too much for it. After two years the Trust supplied them with a small pump powered by a petrol engine and this proved to be most efficient. They never had to use the rainwater available in the tank at the old lighthouse which by now had become derelict.

Frank Williams had no help on the farm at all, except for that of a well-known Manx character, George Quayle, from Lezayre. George Quayle, who is the author of the book *Manx Folklore,* used to stay on the Calf with his daughter for a few days and help to clip the sheep.

Williams quickly came to realise that all the stories that he had heard about the pest of rats and rabbits were true. The island was alive with both. The rats were at first enough to terrify anyone. The Faraghers, like most farmers, had been in the habit of throwing their domestic refuse onto the farm midden not far from the back door, and this had attracted the rats into the yard. When Mrs. Williams opened the back door on the first few mornings she saw to her horror that the rats were advancing towards her. She closed the door rather smartly! Fortunately Warfarin had now been produced as a rat killer. One cannot say poison, for it works in quite a different way. When taken by the rat it has the property of thining the blood. The rat suffers from internal haemorrhage, and literally dies of lethargy, a very humane method of elimination. Williams was most successful with Warfarin. As there were no immune strains on the Calf, he was able to get the entire farm area clear.

Williams, like previous farmers, quickly realised the commercial importance of the rabbits and resolved to harvest this free crop. Working single-handed, however, he was nothing like as successful as his predecessors. It will be recalled that Maddrell once caught 240 in a day, with the help of other men and several dogs. Williams knew nothing of the method employed and decided to use ferrets. The Trust, however, would not allow this. They wisely thought that if the ferrets were to become loose they would interfere with the bird life if they established themselves on the island. Although at that time the Calf was not an official bird observatory, one of Mr. Dickens' reasons for giving the Calf to the National Trust was the hope that some day one would be established. In any case Williams could not use Maddrell's methods of allowing the rabbits to congregate in the pastureland, close up the holes in the walls and then hunt them with dogs, as he had to work alone. Shooting was too slow, and who would buy a rabbit full of shot? The only method left was to snare them. The humane type of wire snare was used, the kind that could not pull completely tight and slowly throttle the rabbit, but only close enough to catch the rabbit by the neck. Williams used to set 200 of these snares every night, a tremendous job for one man. The first morning that he went down to see what he had caught, he was very distressed to find that the "humane" snares had proved to be anything but that. The rabbits had been caught alive alright, but had also been eaten alive, being torn to pieces by the gulls! The only thing to do was to get up each morning before dawn and get to the rabbits before the gulls did. This method of catching rabbits was really uneconomic. Only about twelve a day were caught in spite of the large number of snares. There were so many exits to the warrens that it was quite impossible to trap rabbits that way. The rabbits were shipped to Port St. Mary in sacks and then to Douglas. Sometimes, if the boat could not be used, the rabbits had to be thrown away. Williams suffered another misfortune when the Douglas merchant failed to pay his account! It is interesting to learn that the price of rabbits had by now risen from 1d retail in the Duke of Athol's time to 2/- wholesale in 1954. Inflation has been with us for a long time.

Frank Williams' efforts to profit from the enormous numbers of rabbits were to be shortlived. In 1955 Myxamatosis struck the rabbit population, and in a short time there was scarcely a rabbit to be seen. The rabbits that had thrived on the Calf for 285 years had almost completely disappeared. Williams has a theory which is different from the one which blames the introduction of Myxamatosis to the Calf on a diseased rabbit carcase dropped by a gull. I agree with him that, although gulls sometimes carry and drop the bones, to carry a whole rabbit would be most unlikely. Williams thinks that rabbit fleas were brought over. His white Bull Terrier once caught a diseased rabbit which was found to be alive with red fleas, some of which quickly moved over to the dog's muzzle. His theory is that the fleas were brought over, having been transferred to a gull feeding on a diseased rabbit on the main island and then flying over to the Calf.

After the Williams family had settled in, Frank turned his attention to raising a crop to feed the farm animals. He again consulted Mr. Howie, the Agricultural Officer, who advised him to sow a mixed corn crop, that is to say a mixture of oats, barley, peas, beans, and vetches, which was to be undersown with grass. The mixed corn was to be reaped and eventually placed in the existing stone and concrete silo. With no little difficulty due to inexperience, land nearly opposite the old lighthouses was prepared and the grass and mixed corn sown. The latter grew very well but was never harvested as it was destroyed by the continual bad weather that autumn. Williams was undoubtedly having to learn the hard way. The following year, 1956, he tried two acres of rape. The Calf, like much of the main island, has an acid soil which is quite unsuitable for that crop. He learned this to his cost, for rape proved to be a complete failure.

The failure of the rape was Williams' last effort to grow a crop. He never tried oats which might have done better, especially after the rabbit menace was so fortunately eliminated. In fairness to Frank Williams, who some people might be led to think gave up too easily, it must be realised that the importation of lime was quite out of the question. It would have taken at least three tons to the acre, and, apart from the cost, how could the large quantity which would have been required be shipped over by a small motor boat? In spite of the optimistic suggestion by the Duke of Athol when selling the Calf to the Crown 128 years earlier, it was quite unfeasible.

It would be unfair to compare Williams' results with those of Maddrell forty years before. Maddrell was an experienced farmer and had other help as well as that of at least one son and sometimes two. In any case, Maddrell concentrated his efforts on a few store cattle and his sheep. It is significant that Fred Faragher, also a farmer with lifelong experience, claimed to have lost £2,000, a large sum in those days, during his tenancy of the Calf.

Sheep seem to do well on the Calf. They thrived during the Athol period. Maddrell and Faragher did well with them. Williams' small flock rose to between fifty and sixty, and the little flock of Loaghtan sheep now on the Calf are multiplying. The main problem with sheep is the cliffs; not only do the sheep fall over the steep ones, but they climb down the lesser slopes and find that they cannot return. Everyone from the Athols to Williams suffered losses from this. Williams also lost seventeen sheep from 'Worm' during his last year on the island.

Williams concentrated largely on being self-supporting. Apart from a few sheep and the odd calf or two, he exported nothing but the fleeces. It was surprising to learn that feral goats had appeared again. Maddrell had cleared them out in his day. As Faragher found them in his time, and shot at least six himself, it would seem that goats must have been re-introduced by Robert Mitchell. Williams counted one Billy and six Nannies at one time, and when he finally gave up the farm in 1958 he knew that there were at least three left. On a nostalgic visit with some friends in 1959 he saw a dead one near the silo. None have been seen since.

Mrs. Williams loved her garden. It was Mrs. Williams who planted the cultivated foxgloves that can still be seen. The temperature is slightly higher than that of the main island. Frost is almost unknown, and the rare snow was never more than an inch deep in her time and it melted quickly. Her Scented Geraniums survived the winter outside. Mr. Williams once caught a visitor re-embarking at Cow Harbour with one of these plants that he had stolen during their absence!

The summer visitors were something of a nuisance to the Williams. Under the terms of their contract they had to supply tea and biscuits to anyone who required refreshments. They were frequently called away from their work to do this. Sometimes a whole boatload would arrive at the same time if they were in a party.

The lighthouse restored by Haigh and occupied in Mitchell's time had once again become derelict, as had Jane's House. Williams told a story about Jane's House that he had heard from an old resident of Cregneish. It would seem that Haigh put an advertisement in a Manx paper, for someone prepared to put up with a life on a remote island in order to catch the rabbits. The only applicant lived at Jane's House for about a year, which was in quite good condition then. One day the police went over and took him away. He was, if the story is not apocryphal, a person wanted for murder in Glasgow! Williams, like Maddrell, never saw any sign of the *Keill.*

Transport to the Calf was provided by the Manx Museum and National Trust. There was the *Leprechaun*, an eighteen foot boat with an inboard engine. This was moored in the small dock at Cow Harbour during the summer and hauled up into the boathouse for the winter. There was also a ten foot dinghy, the *Wiggle,* with a Seagull outboard motor. This little boat became a total loss, being smashed by a heavy sea against a rock. The *Wiggle* lacked power and once, on attempting to cross the Sound after the tide had turned, Williams realised that he wasn't going to make it. Being a resourceful character he managed to reach Kitterland, from which after some little time he was ignominiously rescued by a lobster fisherman from Port Erin. Only a retired Royal Navy Lieutenant-Commander who had survived the *Royal Oak* and *Repulse* could tell this story against himself and get away with it!

It is not generally known that the stone barn near the Café at the Sound belongs to the Trust. It is most useful for storing goods awaiting shipment, and in Williams' time even had a telephone. Popplewell's poles from Cregneish have been of some use after all. As the passage across the Sound could only be undertaken at certain states of the tide, the time spent on the mainland had to be reduced to a minimum. After crossing from the Calf, Williams would go to the barn where he kept an old van. Then he used to phone ahead to order all the supplies that he required, so that when he reached Port St. Mary or Castletown his goods would be waiting ready to be picked up.

Frank and Marian Williams had only been on the Calf for two months when they had an experience that neither of them will ever forget, and one that has probably never happened to anyone else either before or since. When the Williams arrived on the Calf for the first time, Marian was expecting their first child. As this happy event was not due until Christmas they did not expect any problems to arise. On November the 29th, although the weather was bad, Frank took Marian across the Sound for the monthly check-up by her doctor. Frank had quite a job crossing the water, and as the weather was most threatening, he decided not to risk being marooned on the main island with the farm animals and the two dogs to feed on the Calf. They re-embarked, and after what seemed like an interminable time managed to get back again. On trying to help to haul up the boat which was rising on the swell even more than usual, Marian slipped and fell. As it did not seem to affect her they thought nothing of it, and were glad to get home again at about five o'clock and eventually went to bed as usual. That night a most violent gale swept the Calf. The needle of the barometer went down right off the scale. Frank still has the paper roll from the barograph at the Port Erin Biological station that was given to him as a souvenir. As the pen on the barograph reached its lowest point at four o'clock in the morning, Marian shook Frank awake and announced that she thought that the baby had started! You can imagine Frank's consternation; there they were marooned alone on an island in a howling gale. Of course, at that time of the year it was pitch black outside, so, apart from making the traditional British cup of tea, there was absolutely nothing that could be done. They didn't even have a light on the tractor. At first light, about 7.30, Frank drove down to the Sound. He could hardly sit on the tractor, and one look at the water told him that it was hopeless. The seas were mountainous and even the lifeboat would have been helpless. Their only chance was a helicopter but they knew that the Isle of Man did not have one stationed there, and in any case could one land in the gale?

The Trust had provided them with twenty hand-held flares to use in an emergency, so Frank thought that the best plan would be to try to signal to the Chickens Rock lighthouse which he knew had a radio-telephone link with the main island. He loaded the flares, some old cloth and canvas, and a tin of paraffin onto the trailer, and set off for the old lighthouses opposite the Chickens Rock light. He unloaded the trailer and tried to light one of the flares, but it seemed to be damp and would not ignite. After several more failures he at last got one to light. As he knew that the lighthouse keepers understood neither Morse nor Sema-phore signals, he waved the flare around trying to spell out the word "Baby"! There was no response, so he tried another flare. Again it failed to ignite. Only three of the twenty flares were of any use. Desperate now, he piled the rags and canvas against the wall, soaked them in paraffin, and after a struggle with the wind at last got them to light. Still no response from the Chickens! He got back on the tractor, raced back to the farm, grabbed a pot of black paint and a brush, and drove back to the lighthouse again. Hardly able to stand up because of the gale, he painted BABY in three foot high letters on the lighthouse wall. The Chickens gave no answering signal. Frank mounted the tractor and drove back home again, dreading what he might find. There was Marian putting in time, calmly sewing a kind of baby's hammock from a piece of old calico which she had designed to slip over the backs of two chairs! Frank then had another idea; he took more rags and paraffin down to the slope facing the main island across the Sound and lit a fire there. He hoped that perhaps it might be seen by someone from Cregneish. He eventually learned that this fire was not seen by anyone, although an hour later when he went down to the Sound again he saw a man and a woman on the other side frantically waving as if they were trying to tell him some-thing. Had any of his signals been seen? If so, could anything be done? He returned to the farm to find Marian quite composed, so he explained the position to her and they prepared to deliver the baby themselves. At 1.45 they heard a strange sound and to their astonishment saw a helicopter land in the field in front of the house!

What had happened was this. The flares were never seen from the Chickens, but the fire at the old lighthouse was seen by a new junior keeper who called the principal keeper. This man realised that there must be trouble of some kind, and this was confirmed when he read through his telescope the word 'BABY'. He contacted the main island and gave the news over his radio-telephone. The lifeboat stations at Port St. Mary and Port Erin were contacted, but both said that it would be impossible to land anyone on the Calf in the gale. The authorities then contacted the Royal Air Force station at Jurby in the North of the Isle of Man, who confirmed that there were no helicopters stationed there. Group Captain Peter Burnett, the Commanding Officer at Jurby, said that if the Fleet Air Arm could send a helicopter he could provide a doctor and an orderly. Very soon after that, a Dragonfly helicopter piloted by Sub-Lieutenant E. G. Meadowcroft of Belfast took off from Eglington, Northern Ireland, with an Avenger plane flying as escort. The helicopter flew to Ronaldsway, the Manx civilian airport, where it picked up the R.A.F. doctor, Squadron Leader A. H. Trench, and took off, landing him on the Calf. The helicopter returned to Ronaldsway and then took over Nurse E. Heath, who was at the time the Superintendent of the Manx Nursing Service. The helicopter, leaving the doctor and wireless operator behind, then flew Mrs. Williams and the Nurse to Ronaldsway, where an R.A.F. ambulance was waiting to take Mrs. Williams to the Douglas Maternity Home. The helicopter then had to make a further trip to the Calf to pick up the doctor and wireless operator. Poor Frank Williams had to be left on the Calf, for he could not leave the farm animals and his two dogs. Shortly after this Marian Williams had her baby, a girl, Sally Elizabeth.

It was a week before the weather allowed Frank to leave the Calf to visit his wife in Douglas, and a further fortnight before Marian and the baby could be smuggled home to escape the crowds of newspaper reporters who made trips to the Calf for weeks afterwards to squeeze out the last bit of news. As one would expect, the national press reported the event in the most sensational way. An amazing story printed in one of the big papers was that the principal keeper on the Chickens Rock light-house, on hearing the news of the birth, ordered a signal rocket to be fired over the Calf with pink stars to tell Frank, "It's a girl!".

The plight of the Williams family marooned on the Calf without means of communication was taken up by Deemster Kneale, who persuaded the Trust to provide the Warden with a radio-telephone of his own. Williams then used to make a regular call to the Douglas Police Station at 9.0 a.m. each day to let them know that all was well.

The Williams reluctantly left the Calf on September 1st, 1958, having lived there for almost exactly four years. Their reason for leaving was Sally. They felt that it was unfair and wrong for her to grow up without other children to play with. There was also the question of her education to be considered. Fortunately Sally suffered no ill effects from the exciting events prior to her premature birth. She proved to be most intelligent; by the time she was four she could read simple words, having been taught by her mother. She later gained a full boarding scholarship to the Buchan School, and is now a tri-lingual secretary.

Frank and Marian Williams did not go to live on the Calf because they thought that they would make their fortune. The salary as warden was almost non-existent, a mere £50 a year, and Frank realised that to make the farm pay would tax the skill of a farmer with a lifetime's experience. It was the remoteness and the complete feeling of peace and tranquillity that attracted them, together with their love of nature and feeling of independence. Their nostalgic feeling for the Calf made them long to return again. Many years later, when Sally was safely boarding at the Buchan School, they made an unofficial enquiry about the possibility of being allowed to live there again. They were disappointed to learn that this was now no longer possible, as in 1962 the Calf had become an official bird observatory. As from that date the ownership of the Calf has remained unchanged and all the Wardens have been ornithologists.

# CHAPTER 10

## ORNITHOLOGY

After Frank Williams had left farming on the Calf finally ceased after two hundred years of increasing difficulty. It had become completely uneconomical.

However, the Calf was to enter into a new period of entirely different history. For many years it had been known that the island was on a migratory route for numerous species of birds, and that many others used it as a breeding place. The Manx Museum and National Trust therefore decided to employ an ornithologist as a warden. They obtained a grant towards the cost from the British Trust for Ornithology and appointed as warden a Norwegian, Einar Brun.

Einar Brun who arrived with his wife, Dido, on April 9th, 1959, quickly realised the importance of the site, for, during the six months' season, he ringed over 3,000 birds of more than sixty species. He was of the opinion that an official observatory should be established, to become a part of the Jersey to Fair Isle chain of similar stations. The old farmhouse, still in excellent condition, would make an ideal headquarters, and might even be adapted to take students.

Einar and Dido Brun, to whom we are indebted for their devoted work and great interest in the Calf, also acted as Wardens during 1960. They had the assistance of several Cambridge students for part of the time. No official Warden was appointed for the 1961 season, but much good work was done by students and other interested persons.

In 1962 the Calf of Man was included in the chain of officially recognised observatories, and another qualified warden was appointed. This was Alan H. Moreley, who manned the station during the two peaks of the migratory season. It was this warden who realised the importance of the old millpond as an attraction for ducks and other birds, and who did so much to improve the dam.

In 1963 Rodney Rayment joined Alan Moreley as warden. This year was notable for the start of the plan to eliminate the rats that were so destructive of the birds and their young. The use of Warfarin for this purpose has continued to the present day.

The 1964 season opened with the same pair of wardens, but Mr. Moreley had to leave, and, for the remainder of that season, Mr. Rayment was the warden, with Henry Smith as his assistant.

The warden for 1965 was P. Bennett assisted by J. Walmsley. They were followed by M. Alexander in 1967. From 1968 up to the time of writing the warden has been the well-known ornithologist, Malcolm Wright.

Being in the centre of the Irish Sea the Calf of Man is, of course, ideally situated as a landfall for migrant birds. These are attracted by the beams of the lighthouse as they fly north in the spring. During the autumn migration they reach the Calf, having followed the coasts of the Isle of Man. The migrants tend to cross the Calf in a direction roughly north and south between The Puddle and Gibbdale Bay. They frequently follow the line of the glen and pass the farm buildings, now the Observatory. For those that land this little valley provides shelter from the weather and some protection from the raptorial birds. There are a number of shrubs, a few trees, and much bracken. The glen also provides an abundance of seeds and insect life upon which to feed.

This concentration of migrants is of great help to the warden, who sets most of his traps and nets on this known migratory line. The nets are called Mistnets, and are not unlike a Badminton net, made of fine nylon with a continuous horizontal pocket. When set against a dark background they are almost invisible. The birds strike the net and fall into the pocket quite unharmed, and there await collection. The great disadvantage of the Mistnet is that it cannot be used in bad weather. Several other forms of traps are used, the Heligoland trap being the most successful. This trap is made of wire netting, and is shaped like an unspillable inkwell with a central funnel. It works rather like a lobster-pot. Of the thousands of birds caught each season, about two-thirds are caught in the Mistnets.

When the birds are caught they are carefully placed, head first, into small, separate cloth bags of known weight. They are then weighed on a small spring balance to an accuracy of one tenth of a gram. The wings are measured to the nearest millimetre, as are the tail, the tarsus bone of the leg, and the beak. The sex of the bird is also recorded, together with information about the bird's age, i.e. whether it is a juvenile or an adult. The birds are sometimes examined for ectoparasites. Before being released through a small hatch in the Observatory window, the birds are ringed with a numbered ring. This is fastened round the leg by means of a special type of pliers. The number of the ring and all other details are ultimately sent to the British Museum, London. Since 1959 over 52,000 birds have been ringed in this way.

Ringing is perhaps the most important part of the work, for, once ringed and recorded, the bird becomes an individual among the myriad numbers of its species. Thus migratory routes can be marked on maps, together with the bird's breeding places and winter quarters. For instance, a Chiffchaff ringed on the Calf was caught in Gambia, West Africa. The speed of flight during migration can also be determined.

Sometimes the gales blow the migrants many hundreds of miles off course; this is known as a "drift migration". It is not unknown for American birds for instance to be blown right across the Atlantic. In 1971 the Calf had just such an unusual visitor. It was an American Song Sparrow, *Melospiza melodia*. This interesting bird was caught in a Heligoland trap, and, after being recorded and released, was seen to feed on various grass seeds. It was seen again several times during the next fornight. It was thought that this particular bird, because of the excellent condition of its plumage, may have hitched a lift on a boat for part of its long journey. It is, of course, not unknown for exhausted birds to land on ships and rest there for a few days.

Among the birds that have been known to nest on the Calf are the following. It is not claimed that this list is complete in any way.

| | |
|---|---|
| *Turdus merula* | Blackbird |
| *Fringilla coelebs* | Chaffinch |
| *Pyrrhacorax pyrrhacorax* | Chough |
| *Phalacrocorax carbo* | Cormorant |
| *Cuculus canorus* | Cuckoo |
| *Prucella modularis* | Dunnock |
| *Fulmarus glacialis* | Fulmar |
| *Locustella naevia* | Grasshopper Warbler |
| *Larus marinus* | Great Black-Backed Gull |
| *Uria aalge* | Guillemot |
| *Larus argentatus* | Herring Gull |
| *Corvus corone cornix* | Hooded Crow |
| *Passer domesticus* | House Sparrow |
| *Falco tinnunculus* | Kestrel |
| *Rissa tridactyla* | Kittiwake |
| *Vanellus vanellus* | Lapwing |
| *Larus fuscus* | Lesser Black-Backed Gull |
| *Carduelis cannabina* | Linnet |
| *Pica pica* | Magpie |
| *Anas platyrhynchos* | Mallard |
| *Anthus pratensis* | Meadow Pipit |
| *Turdus viscivorus* | Mistle Thrush |
| *Gallinula chloropus* | Moorhen |
| *Haematopus ostralegus* | Oystercatcher |
| *Perdix perdix* | Partridge |
| *Fratercula arctica* | Puffin |
| *Corvus corax* | Raven |
| *Alca torda* | Razorbill |
| *Emberiza schoeniclus* | Reed Bunting |
| *Erithacus rubecula* | Robin |
| *Anthus spinoletta* | Rock Pipit |
| *Acrocephalus schoenobaenus* | Sedge Warbler |
| *Phalacrocorax aristotelis* | Shag |
| *Asio flammeus* | Short-Eared Owl |
| *Alauda arvensis* | Skylark |

| | |
|---|---|
| *Muscicapa striata* | Spotted Flycatcher |
| *Sturnus vulgaris* | Starling |
| *Saxicola torquata* | Stonechat |
| *Hirundo rustica* | Swallow |
| *Oenanthe oenanthe* | Wheatear |
| *Sylvia communis* | Whitethroat |
| *Columba palumbus* | Wood Pigeon |
| *Troglodytes troglodytes* | Wren |

One would like to include the Manx Shearwater in the list, but its return to the Calf, though probable, is yet to be proved.

Other sea birds of the eleven species that are included nest in their thousands. The Herring Gull, as one would expect, is by far the most common of these. The Cormorants nest on the north-east cliffs and also on the Stack. The Shag is mostly to be found on Kione Ny Halby, while the Fulmar breeds on both the north-east and west of the island. In addition to its nests on the Calf, the Great Black-backed Gull also breeds on Kitterland. The Burroo is also a favourite nesting site for several species of sea birds, including the Guillemot.

When the Chickens Rock lighthouse was replaced by a new one on the Calf itself, it was hoped that the migration over the island would not be interfered with, and this fortunately has proved to be the case. If, as is believed, the lighthouse influences and guides the birds on their flight, we are most fortunate, for the new light is much more powerful than the old one.

The new lighthouse was first illuminated in July, 1968. During the early part of that year's autumn migration the light had little effect, but once the longer nights of October arrived, it became evident that its influence would be as great as, if not greater than, that of the old one on the Chickens. In clear weather the light now has a range of twenty-three miles.

In the space of a few days thousands of birds were seen, the species most numerous at that time being Blackbirds, Redwings, Thrushes, and Fieldfares. In the early hours of the morning Mr. Wright estimated that there were about a thousand flying round the tower in the direction of the rotating light, but always just above it. A few ignored the one-way traffic and flew around the wrong way! Only a few fluttered against the glass, most circling well out from the tower which is only about thirty feet high. The extremely bright light seemed to prevent the birds from colliding with the glass, a tragedy which happens so frequently with isolated tower lights of lesser brilliance. On searching the ground around the tower each morning, Mr. Wright was relieved to find that, as far as he could tell, no birds had been killed.

The number of species of birds known to have visited the Calf is over a hundred and twenty. These include the forty species known to have nested there. A bird sanctuary indeed, and one that owes its success to its generous donor, the officials of the Manx Museum and National Trust, and the devoted and highly skilled work of the various Wardens.

# Bibliography

*The Athol Papers.* Manx Museum Library.

Blundell, William. *A History of the Isle of Man,* 1648/56. The Manx Society, Volume XXV, Part I, 1876. The Manx Society, Volume XXVII, Part II, 1877.

*The Bridgehouse Papers.* Manx Museum Library.

*The Brig Lily Disaster.* The Manx Museum. B.158-3.

Bruce, J. R. *Manx Archaeological Survey, 6th Report.*

Brun, Einar. *Recent Contributions to Manx Ornithology.* Journal of the Manx Museum 1959/60.

Bushell, Thomas. The Superlative Prodigal. *The First Part of Youths Errors,* 1628. British Library, 851.F. 38.

Bushell, Thomas. *Mineral Overtures to Parliament.* Included in *Mr. Bushell's Abridgement of the Lord Chancellor Bacon's Philosophical theory in Mineral Prosecutions.* British Library, shelf mark 7.19405.

*The Calf of Man Bird Observatory Reports.* Bird Study Volume 20 no. 4.

Camden, William. *Britannia,* 1777, Printed for W. Bower, London.

*Castletown Deeds,* No. II. 1829 No. 9. The Manx Museum.

Chaloner, James. *A Short Treaties of the Isle of Man,* 1656. S. Tymms, Lowestoft, reprinted 1864.

Clay, Charles. *Currency of the Isle of Man.* The Manx Society, Volume XVII, 1869.

Cubbon, W. M. *Island Heritage.* G. Falknery and Sons Ltd., Manchester, 1952.

Cummings, J. G. *Geology of the Calf of Man.* The Proceedings of the Geological Society, London, 1847.

Cummings, J. G. *The Isle of Man.* Edward Stanforth, 1861.

De La Pryne. *The Recluse on the Calf.* The Manx Society, Volume XXX, 1880.

*The Dictionary of National Biography.* Volume 8, Re: Thomas Bushell.

*The Domestic Calendars of Charles II.* Included in *The Calendars of State Papers Domestic.* Published by the Public Record Office. (The British Library.)

*Episcopal Wills and Administration, 1800-1884.* In the General Registry, Douglas.

Feltham, John. *A Tour through the Isle of Mann in 1797 and 1798.* R. Crutwell, 1798.

Fraser, Maxwell. *In Praise of Manxland.* Methuen and Company, 2nd edn., 1948.

Garrad, Larch S. *The Naturalist in the Isle of Man.* David and Charles, 1972.

Gough, J. W. *The Superlative Prodigal.* J. W. A. Brown and Smith Limited, Bristol, 1932.

Hague, Douglas B. *The Building on the Summit of the Calf of Man.* The Calf of Man Bird Observatory Report, 1971.

Kendall, Percy F. *The Glacial Survey of the Isle of Man.* Manchester Lit. & Phil. Society, 1891.

Kinvig, R. H. *A History of the Isle of Man.* Oxford University Press, 1944.

Kneen, J. J. *Manx Personal Names.* The Manx Museum and Ancient Monuments Trustees, 1937.

La Mothe, A. E. *Manx Yarns.* The Manx Sun Limited, 1905.

Lamplough, G. W. *The Geology of the Isle of Man.* H.M. Stationery Office, 1903.

*Liber Assedationis.* In the Library of the Manx Museum.

*Liber Cancheller.* In the Library of the Manx Museum.

Megaw, B. R. S. *The Crucifixion Slab.* Journal of the Manx Museum, Volume 6.

Moore, A. W. *The Folklore of the Isle of Man,* 1891. Douglas Brown and Sons, Douglas.

Northern Lighthouse Board. *The Calf of Man Lighthouse.* Edinburgh, 1968.

Nelson, Esther. *The Island Penitent.* Island Minstrels and G.B., Whittaker, Liverpool, 1839.

The Proceedings of the Isle of Man Natural History and Antiquarian Society.

Quayle, George. *Manx Folklore.* Courier/Herald. Douglas, 1973.

Quayle, John. (attributed to) *A Description of the Several Parishes of the Isle of Man,* 1775. Among the Bridgehouse Papers.

Robertson, David. *A Tour Through the Isle of Man,* 1794. Printed for the author by E. Hodson.

Roeder, C. *Thomas Bushell and his Seclusion on the Calf.* Manx Notes and Queries. S. & C. Broadbent and Company, Douglas.
Rodgers, H.M. *Bird Life on the Calf.* Journal of the Manx Museum, Volume 3.
*The Sheading Roll.* In the Library of the Manx Museum.
*Sir Henry Ellis's Original Letters of Illustrated English History.* London, 1824. (The British Library.)
*The Statutes of the Isle of Man 1417-1824.*
Stenning, Rev. *Isle of Man.* Robert Hale Ltd., 1950.
Stenning, Rev. *A Portrait of the Isle of Man.* Robert Hale Ltd., 1958.
Townley, Richard. *A Journal Kept in the Isle of Man.* J. Ware and Son, 1791.
Train, Joseph. *An Historical and Statistical Account of the Isle of Man.* Mary A. Quiggin, Douglas, 1845. In two volumes.
*Various Deeds of the Drinkwater Family.* In the General Registry, Douglas.
*A Valuation and Report on the Isle of Man.* The Athol Papers. Manx Museum.
Waldron, George. *A Description of the Isle of Man,* 1726. Reprinted in Manx Society Volume XI, 1865.
Williamson, Kenneth. *Ornithology of the Calf of Man.* Natural History and Antiquarian Society, 1940.
Williamson, Kenneth. *Puffins on the Calf Isle.* Journal of the Manx Museum, Volume 4, 1940.
Woods, George. *An Account of the Past and Present State of the Isle of Man.* Robert Baldwin, London, 1811.

*Maps*

Blaeu 1645
Captain G. Collins 1693
John Drinkwater 1826
Peter Fannin 1789
Geological Survey 1892/97
Manx Museum Archaeological Map
Mercator 1564
Ordnance Survey 1869
Speed 1605, 1610
Commander G. Williams 1847
Richard D. Wilson 1771

*Newspapers filed in the Manx Museum Library*
The Advertiser
The Gazette
The Isle of Man Weekly Times
The Manx Sun

# Index

## E

Eoch, 28.
Earl of Buchan, 11.
Eggs, 69, 75, 79.
Electric light, 73, 76.
Emergency signal, 70.
Emilia (smack), 35.
English Crown, 64.
Exchequer Book, 56.
Extra parochial, 64.
Eye, 8.

## F

Fairfax, General Lord, 44.
Fairies, 27.
Fanning, Peter, 62.
Faragher, Frederick James, 76, 77, 79, 82.
Farm buildings, 64, 71, 89.
Feather gathering, 44, 62.
Felspar, 41.
Feltham, John, 62.
Fenced-in land, 60, 67, 72.
Ferries, 65.
Ferry house, 65.
Flares, 84.
Fog, 36, 40, 41.
Forbes, D., 60
Fortifications, 20, 56.
Frazer, Maxwell, 57.

## G

Gably, Capt. S., 21, 23, 24.
Garden, 34, 82.
Garrett, Robert, 73, 74, 75.
George (schooner), 35.
Ghaw Kione Dhoo, 27.
Giau, 8.
Giau Lang, 8.
Giau Yiarn, 8.
Gibbdale Bay, 8, 9, 12, 47, 89.
Glacial Drift, 11.
Glacial Striae, 11.
Goats, feral, 50, 82.
Godred Crovan I, 55.
Goll, 8.
Goll-ny-Staggy, 8.
Goll-ny-Vurroo, 8, 36.
Gourley, John, 62, 63.
Governor (The), 37, 44, 73.
Granite, 11.
Grants harbour, 7, 8.
Gravel pit, 11.
Graves, 14, 70.
Grits, 11.
Ground rent, 44.

## H

Hague, Douglas B., 14.
Haigh, Samuel, 50, 67, 68, 69, 70, 71, 79, 83.
Heligoland Trap, 89, 90.
Hermits, 13, 15, 16.
Humphrey, John, 60.

## I

Irish wherries, 23.
Iter Lancastrense, 17.

## J

James, Rev. Richard, 17.
Jane's House, 9, 10, 14, 15, 40, 49, 62, 70, 71, 83.
Jeanne St. Charles (ship), 39.
Jersey to Fair Isle chain of Observatories, 87.

## K

Keill, 13, 14, 19, 70, 83.
Kelly, Harry, 69.
King Charles I, 18.
King Charles II, 19.
King Edward I, 11.
King Edward III, 43.
King James, 17.
King Olaf, 27.
Kinvig, Professor R. H., 15.
Kione-ny-Halby, 47.
Kitter, 8, 27.
Kitterland, 8, 11, 12, 27, 28, 36, 37, 62, 64, 83.

## L

Lascars, 40, 71.
Latin inscription, 66.
Lazybeds, 12.
Lead, 11.
Leases, 60, 61, 62, 64.
Le Calf, 7, 56.
Liber Assedationis, 56.
Lifeboats, 32, 42.
Lighthouse keepers, 9, 12, 63, 64, 66, 70, 84.
Lighthouses, 7, 9, 12, 29, 30, 32, 33, 34, 68, 70, 71, 75, 80, 83, 84, 89, 91.
Lily (brig) disaster, 36, 37, 39.
Lime kiln, 9.
Lintel graves, 14.
Lion (brig), 35.
Loaghtan sheep, 50, 59, 82.
Lode, 12.
Longboats, 43.
Look-out place, 19.
Lord Chancellor, 16.
Lord's Rent, 56.
Lordship of Mann, 55.
Lorrimer, Mr., 63.
Ludwidge, Mr., 29.
Luggers, 35.
Lyndsay, Governor, 59, 60.

Sheep, 40, 50, 56, 57, 58, 59, 60, 62, 63, 64, 67, 68, 71, 74, 77, 78, 80, 82.
Shepherd, Mr., 65, 66.
Shepherds, 59, 62, 66.
Shepherd's hut, 62.
Sheshaght ny Kiree Loaghtan, 51.
Shopping, 79.
Signal Station, 70.
Silo, 70, 71, 81.
Skeealyn, 25.
Skerries, 30.
Skerryvore, 33.
Skokholm, 46.
Slate, 10, 11.
Smacks, 35.
Small, Capt. G., 30.
Smithy, 9, 70.
Smugglers, 8.
Snares, 81.
Soil, 81.
Sound, 7, 8, 11, 27, 28, 35, 36, 39, 40, 41, 68, 75, 83.
South Harbour, 7, 9, 12, 13, 61, 68, 70, 71.
Spanish Head, 39.
Spar, 10.
Speed, 14.
Spottiswood, John, 31.
Springs, 68, 70.
Stack, 8.
Stakkr, 8.
Stanleys, 12, 55.
Stevensons, 17, 44, 55, 56.
Stone barn (at Sound), 83.
Stone walls, 15, 60.
Store houses, 65.
Sugarloaf Rock, 8.
Summers, John, 62.
Swell, 8.
Syenites, 11.

**T**

Taxes, 67.
Telephone, 72, 75, 83.
Temperature, 70.
The Crucifixion Slab, 15.
The Isle of Man, 10.
Thouᶜla, 8, 39.
Thie Vushell, 19.
Tholtan, 49.
Tides, 7.
Tithe, 44, 63, 64.
Tourist attraction, 73.
Tourists, 65, 75, 82.
Townley, Richard, 10, 47.
Tractors, 76, 78, 80.
Trailer, 78, 80.
Train, Joseph, 7, 15, 50, 66.

Traps (bird), 89, 90.
Tremouille, Charlotte de la, 44.
Trinity House, 30,
Turf, 23.

**U**

U-boats, 71.

**V**

Vadrill Onny, 25.
Valley, 9, 89.
Veins of metal, 11.
Victoria (lugger), 35.
Vikings, 50.

**W**

Waldron, George, 44, 57.
Wardens, 41, 74, 76, 77, 87, 89, 91.
Wharf, 71, 79.
Water supply, 72, 80.
Williamson, K., 74.
Williams, Lt.-Cmdr. Frank, 77, 78, 79, 80, 81, 82, 83, 84, 85, 86, 87.
Willoughby, Francis, 45.
Wilson, Bishop, 44, 45.
Wilson, Richard D., 9, 29.
Windvane, 67, 73.
Wood's Atlas, 66.
Woods, George, 19, 27, 47, 62.
World War I, 70.
World War II, 75, 76.
Wrack, 57, 91.
Wrecks, 35.
Wright, Malcolm, 89.

**X   Y   Z**

Yn Calloo, 7.
Yn Keelis, 7.
Yn Kellagh, 7.
Young Halliday (ship), 36.